Your
Horoscope
2014

Libra

Your Personal Horoscope 2014

Libra

24th September–23rd October

igloobooks

igloobooks

Published in 2013 by Igloo Books Ltd
Cottage Farm
Sywell
Northants
NN6 0BJ
www.igloobooks.com

Produced for Igloo Books by W. Foulsham & Co. Ltd, Capital Point, 33 Bath Road, Slough, Berkshire, SL1 3UF, England

HUN001 0713
2 4 6 8 10 9 7 5 3 1
ISBN: 978-1-78197-580-0

This is an abridged version of material originally published in Old Moore's Horoscope and Astral Diary.

Printed and manufactured in China

CONTENTS

1	Introduction	7
2	The Essence of Libra: Exploring the Personality of Libra the Scales	9
3	Libra on the Cusp	15
4	Libra and its Ascendants	17
5	The Moon and the Part it Plays in your Life	31
6	Moon Signs	35
7	Libra in Love	39
8	Venus: The Planet of Love	43
9	Venus through the Zodiac Signs	45
10	Libra: 2013 Diary Pages	49
11	Libra: 2014 Diary Pages	71
12	Libra: 2014 In Brief	72
13	Rising Signs for Libra	157
14	The Zodiac, Planets and Correspondences	159

INTRODUCTION

Your Personal Horoscopes have been specifically created to allow you to get the most from astrological patterns and the way they have a bearing on not only your zodiac sign, but nuances within it. Using the diary section of the book you can read about the influences and possibilities of each and every day of the year. It will be possible for you to see when you are likely to be cheerful and happy or those times when your nature is in retreat and you will be more circumspect. The diary will help to give you a feel for the specific 'cycles' of astrology and the way they can subtly change your day-to-day life. For example, when you see the sign ☿, this means that the planet Mercury is retrograde at that time. Retrograde means it appears to be running backwards through the zodiac. Such a happening has a significant effect on communication skills, but this is only one small aspect of how the Personal Horoscope can help you.

With Your Personal Horoscope the story doesn't end with the diary pages. It includes simple ways for you to work out the zodiac sign the Moon occupied at the time of your birth, and what this means for your personality. In addition, if you know the time of day you were born, it is possible to discover your Ascendant, yet another important guide to your personal make-up and potential.

Many readers are interested in relationships and in knowing how well they get on with people of other astrological signs. You might also be interested in the way you appear to very different sorts of individuals. If you are such a person, the section on Venus will be of particular interest. Despite the rapidly changing position of this planet, you can work out your Venus sign, and learn what bearing it will have on your life.

Using Your Personal Horoscope you can travel on one of the most fascinating and rewarding journeys that anyone can take – the journey to a better realisation of self.

THE ESSENCE OF LIBRA

Exploring the Personality of Libra the Scales

(24TH SEPTEMBER – 23RD OCTOBER)

What's in a sign?

At heart you may be the least complicated of all the zodiac sign types, though your ruling element is Air, and that is always going to supply some surprises. Diplomatic, kind and affectionate, your nature blows like a refreshing breeze through the lives of almost anyone you meet. It isn't like you to be gloomy for very long at a time, and you know how to influence the world around you.

It's true that you don't like dirt, or too much disorganisation, and you tend to be very artistic by inclination. You get your own way in life, not by dint of making yourself unpopular in any way but rather with the sort of gentle persuasion to which almost everyone you know falls victim at one time or another. Being considerate of others is more or less second nature to you, though you may not be quite as self-sacrificing as sometimes appears to be the case. You definitely know what you want from life and are not above using a little subterfuge when it comes to getting it.

You are capable and resourceful, but just a little timid on occasions. All the same, when dealing with subject matter that you know and relish, few can better you out there in the practical world. You know how to order your life and can be just as successful in a career sense as you tend to be in your home life. There are times when personal attractions can be something of a stumbling block because you love readily and are very influenced by the kindness and compliments of those around you.

Librans do need to plan ahead, but don't worry about this fact too much because you are also extremely good at thinking on your feet. Getting others to do your bidding is a piece of cake because you are not tardy when it comes to showing your affections. Nevertheless you need to be careful not to allow yourself to fall into unreliable company, or to get involved in schemes that seem too good to be true – some of them are. But for most of the time you present a happy picture to the world and get along just fine, with your ready smile and adaptable personality. You leave almost any situation happier and more contented than it was when you arrived.

Libra resources

When it comes to getting on in life you have as much ammunition in your armoury as most zodiac signs and a great deal more than some. For starters you are adaptable and very resourceful. When you have to take a leap in logic there is nothing preventing you from doing so, and the strong intuition of which your zodiac sign is capable can prove to be very useful at times.

One of your strongest points is the way you manage to make others love you. Although you might consider yourself to be distinctly 'ordinary', that's not the way the world at large perceives you. Most Librans have the ability to etch themselves onto the minds of practically everyone they come across. Why? It's simple. You listen to what people have to say and appear to be deeply interested. On most occasions you are, but even if the tale is a tedious one you give the impression of being rooted to the spot with a determination to hear the story right through. When it comes to responding you are extremely diplomatic and always manage to steer a sensible course between any two or more opposing factions.

Having said that you don't like dirt or untidy places, this is another fact that you can turn to your advantage, because you can always find someone who will help you out. So charming can Libra be that those who do all they can to make you more comfortable regularly end up feeling that you have done them a favour.

It is the sheer magic of the understated Libran that does the trick every time. Even on those rare occasions when you go out with all guns blazing to get what you want from life, you are very unlikely to make enemies on the way. Of course you do have to be careful on occasions, like everyone, but you can certainly push issues further than most. Why? Mainly because people don't realise that you are doing so.

You could easily sell any commodity – though it might be necessary to believe in it yourself first. Since you can always see the good points in anything and tend to be generally optimistic, that should not be too problematical either.

Beneath the surface

In many respects Libra could be the least complicated sign of the zodiac so it might be assumed that 'what you see is what you get'. Life is rarely quite that simple, though you are one of the most straightforward people when it comes to inner struggle. The fact is that most Librans simply don't have a great deal. Between subconscious motivation and in-your-face action there is a seamless process. Librans do need to be loved and this fact can be quite a strong motivation in itself towards any particular course of action. However, even this desire for affection isn't the most powerful factor when considering the sign of the Scales.

What matters most to you is balance, which is probably not at all surprising considering what your zodiac sign actually means. Because of this you would go to tremendous lengths to make sure that your inner resolves create the right external signs and actions to offer the peace that you are looking for most of all.

Like most people born under the Air signs you are not quite as confident as you sometimes appear to be. In the main you are modest and not given to boasting, so you don't attract quite the level of attention of your fellow Air signs, Gemini and Aquarius. All the same you are quite capable of putting on an act when it's necessary to give a good account of yourself in public. You could be quaking inside but you do have the ability to hide this from the world at large.

Librans exhibit such a strong desire to be kind to everyone they meet that they may hide their inner feelings from some people altogether. It's important to remember to be basically honest, even if that means upsetting others a little. This is the most difficult trait for Libra to deal with and may go part of the way to explaining why so many relationship break-ups occur for people born under this zodiac sign. However, as long as you find ways and means to explain your deepest emotional needs, at least to those you love, all should be well.

In most respects you tend to be an open book, particularly to those who take the trouble to look. Your nature is not over-deep, and you are almost certainly not on some secret search to find the 'real you'. Although Libra is sometimes accused of being superficial there are many people in the world who would prefer simplicity to complications and duplicity.

Making the best of yourself

This may be the easiest category by far for the zodiac sign of Libra. The fact is that you rarely do anything else but offer the best version of what you are. Presentation is second nature to Libra, which just loves to be noticed. Despite this you are naturally modest and so not inclined to go over the top in company. You can be relied upon to say and do the right things for most of the time. Even when you consider your actions to be zany and perhaps less acceptable, this is not going to be the impression that the majority of people would get.

In a work sense you need to be involved in some sort of occupation that is clean, allows for a sense of order and ultimately offers the ability to use your head as well as your hands. The fact is that you don't care too much for unsavoury sorts of work and need to be in an environment that suits your basically refined nature. If the circumstances are right you can give a great deal to your work and will go far. Librans also need to be involved with others because they are natural co-operators. For this reason you may not be at your best when working alone or in situations that necessitate all the responsibilities being exclusively yours.

When in the social mainstream you tend to make the best of yourself by simply being what you naturally are. You don't need frills and fancies. Libra is able to make the best sort of impression by using the natural qualities inherent in the sign. As a result, your natural poise, your ability to cut through social divisions, your intelligence and your adaptability should all ensure that you remain popular.

What may occasionally prove difficult is being quite as dominant as the world assumes you ought to be. Many people equate efficiency with power. This is not the way of people born under the Scales, and you need to make that fact plain to anyone who seems to have the desire to shape you.

The impressions you give

Although the adage 'what you see is what you get' may be truer for Libra than for any of its companion signs, it can't be exclusively the case. However, under almost all circumstances you are likely to make friends. You are a much shrewder operator than sometimes appears to be the case and tend to weigh things in the balance very carefully. Libra can be most things to most people, and that's the sort of adaptability that ensures success at both a social and a professional level.

The chances are that you are already well respected and deeply liked by most of the people you know. This isn't so surprising since you are not inclined to make waves of any sort. Whether or not this leads to you achieving the degree of overall success that you deserve in life is quite a different matter. When impressions count you don't tend to let yourself down, or the people who rely on you. Adapting yourself to suit different circumstances is the meat and drink of your basic nature and you have plenty of poise and charm to disarm even the most awkward of people.

In affairs of the heart you are equally adept at putting others at their ease. There is very little difficulty involved in getting people to show their affection for you and when it comes to romance you are one of the most successful practitioners to be found anywhere. The only slight problem in this area of life, as with others, is that you are so talented at offering people what they want that you might not always be living the sort of life that genuinely suits you. Maybe giving the right impression is a little too important for Libra. A deeper form of honesty from the start would prevent you from having to show a less charming side to your nature in the end.

In most circumstances you can be relied upon to exhibit a warm, affectionate, kind, sincere and interesting face to the world at large. As long as this underpins truthfulness it's hard to understand how Libra could really go far wrong.

The way forward

You must already be fairly confident that you have the necessary skills and natural abilities to get on well in a world that is also filled with other people. From infancy most Librans learn how to rub along with others, whilst offering every indication that they are both adaptable and amenable to change. Your chameleon-like ability to 'change colour' in order to suit prevailing circumstances means that you occasionally drop back to being part of the wallpaper in the estimation of at least some people. A greater ability to make an impression probably would not go amiss sometimes, but making a big fuss isn't your way and you actively seek an uncomplicated sort of life.

Balance is everything to Libra, a fact that means there are times when you end up with nothing at all. What needs to be remembered is that there are occasions when everyone simply has to make a decision. This is the hardest thing in the world for you to do but when you manage it you become even more noticed by the world at large.

There's no doubt that people generally hold you in great affection. They know you to be quite capable and love your easy-going attitude to life. You are rarely judgmental and tend to offer almost anyone the benefit of the doubt. Although you are chatty, and inclined to listen avidly to gossip, it isn't your natural way to be unkind, caustic or backbiting. As a result it would seem that you have all the prerequisites to live an extremely happy life. Alas, things are rarely quite that easy.

It is very important for you to demonstrate to yourself, as well as to others, that you are an individual with thoughts and feelings of your own. So often do you defer to the needs of those around you that the real you gets somewhat squashed on the way. There have to be times when you are willing to say 'yes' or 'no' unequivocally, instead of a noncommittal 'I don't really mind' or 'whatever you think best'. At the end of the day you do have opinions and can lead yourself into the path of some severe frustrations if you are unwilling to voice them in the first place.

Try to be particularly honest in deep, emotional attachments. Many Libran relationships come to grief simply because there isn't enough earthy honesty present in the first place. People knowing how you feel won't make them care for you any less. A fully integrated, truthful Libran, with a willingness to participate in the decision making, turns out to be the person who is both successful and happy.

LIBRA ON THE CUSP

Astrological profiles are altered for those people born at either the beginning or the end of a zodiac sign, or, more properly, on the cusps of a sign. In the case of Libra this would be on the 24th of September and for two or three days after, and similarly at the end of the sign, probably from the 21st to the 23rd of October.

The Virgo Cusp – September 24th to 26th

On the Cusp does not apply when born 1st October.

Here we find a Libran subject with a greater than average sense of responsibility and probably a better potential for success than is usually the case for Libra when taken alone. The Virgoan tendency to take itself rather too seriously is far less likely when the sign is mixed with Libra and the resultant nature is often very inspiring, and yet quite centred. The Virgo-cusp Libra has what it takes to break through the red tape of society, and yet can understand the need for its existence in the first place. You are [illegible] concerned, quick on the uptake and very ready to listen to any point of view but, at the end of the day, you know when it is going to be necessary to take a personal stance and this you are far more willing to do than would be the case for non-cuspal Librans.

Family members are important to you, but you always allow them their own individuality and don't get in the way of their personal need to spread their [illegible] times when it's hard to take this positive stance. Practically speaking you are a good home maker but you also enjoy travelling and can benefit greatly from seeing the way other cultures think and behave. It is true that you can have the single-mindedness of a Virgoan, but even this aspect is modified by the Libran within you, so that you usually try to see alternative points of view and often succeed in doing so.

At work you really come into your own. Not only are you capable enough to deal with just about any eventuality, you are also willing to be flexible and to make up your mind instantly when it proves necessary to do so. Colleagues and subordinates alike tend to trust you. You may consider self-employment, unlike most Librans who are usually very worried by this prospect. Making your way in life is something you tend to take for granted, even when the going gets tough.

What people most like about you is that, despite your tremendously practical approach to life, you can be very zany and retain a sense of fun that is, at its best, second to none. Few people find you difficult to understand or to get on with in a day-to-day sense.

The Scorpio Cusp – October 21st to 23rd

The main difference between this cusp and the one at the Virgo end of Libra, is that you tend to be more emotionally motivated and of a slightly less practical nature. Routines are easy for you to address, though you can become very restless and tend to find your own emotional responses difficult to deal with. Sometimes even you don't understand what makes you tick, and that can be a problem. Actually you are not as complicated as you may have come to believe. It's simply that you have a unique view of life and one that doesn't always match that of the people around you, but as Libra instinctively wants to conform, this can lead to some personal confusion.

In family matters you are responsible, very caring and deeply committed to others. It's probable that you work in some field that finds you in direct contact with the public at large and many Scorpio-cusp Librans choose welfare, social or hospital work as a first choice. When it comes to love, you are flexible in your choice and the necessary attributes to promote a long-lasting and happy relationship are clearly present in your basic nature. If there are problems, they may come about as a result of your inability to choose properly in the first place, because you are the first to offer anyone the benefit of the doubt.

When it comes to the practicalities of life, Scorpio can prove to be extremely useful. It offers an 'edge' to your nature and, as Scorpio is a Fixed sign, you are less likely to lose ground because of lack of confidence than Libra alone would be. Your future can be bright, but only if you are willing to get involved in something that really interests you in the first place. You certainly do not care for getting your hands dirty and tend to gravitate towards more refined positions.

Creative potential is good and you could be very artistic, though if this extends to fine art, at least some of your pictures will have 'dark' overtones that might shock some people, including yourself. At base you are kind, caring, complicated, yet inspiring.

LIBRA AND ITS ASCENDANTS

The nature of every individual on the planet is composed of the rich variety of zodiac signs and planetary positions that were present at the time of their birth. Your Sun sign, which in your case is Libra, is one of the many factors when it comes to assessing the unique person you are. Probably the most important consideration, other than your Sun sign, is to establish the zodiac sign that was rising over the eastern horizon at the time that you were born. This is your Ascending or Rising sign. Most popular astrology fails to take account of the Ascendant, and yet its importance remains with you from the very moment of your birth, through every day of your life. The Ascendant is evident in the way you approach the world, and so, when meeting a person for the first time, it is this astrological influence that you are most likely to notice first. Our Ascending sign essentially represents what we appear to be, while the Sun sign is what we feel inside ourselves.

The Ascendant also has the potential for modifying our overall nature. For example, if you were born at a time of day when Libra was passing over the eastern horizon (this would be around the time of dawn) then you would be classed as a double Libran. As such, you would typify this zodiac sign, both internally and in your dealings with others. However, if your Ascendant sign turned out to be a Water sign, such as Pisces, there would be a profound alteration of nature, away from the expected qualities of Libra.

One of the reasons why popular astrology often ignores the Ascendant is that it has always been rather difficult to establish. We have found a way to make this possible by devising an easy-to-use table, which you will find on page 157 of this book. Using this, you can establish your Ascendant sign at a glance. You will need to know your rough time of birth, then it is simply a case of following the instructions.

For those readers who have no idea of their time of birth it might be worth allowing a good friend, or perhaps your partner, to read through the section that follows this introduction. Someone who deals with you on a regular basis may easily discover your Ascending sign, even though you could have some difficulty establishing it for yourself. A good understanding of this component of your nature is essential if you want to be aware of that 'other person' who is responsible for the way you make contact with the world at large. Your Sun sign, Ascendant sign, and the other pointers in this book will, together, allow you a far better understanding of what makes you tick as an individual. Peeling back the different layers of your astrological make-up can be an enlightening experience, and the Ascendant may represent one of the most important layers of all.

Libra with Libra Ascendant

There is no doubt that you carry the very best of all Libran worlds in your nature, though at the same time there is a definite possibility that you often fall between two stools. The literal advice as a result is that you must sometimes make a decision, even though it isn't all that easy for you to do so. Not everyone understands your easy-going side and there are occasions when you could appear to be too flippant for your own good.

The way you approach the world makes you popular, and there is no doubt at all that you are the most diplomatic person to be found anywhere in the length and breadth of the zodiac. It is your job in life to stop people disagreeing and since you can always see every point of view, you make a good impression on the way.

Relationships can sometimes be awkward for you because you can change your mind so easily. But love is never lacking and you can be fairly certain of a generally happy life. Over-indulging is always a potential problem for Air-sign people such as yourself, and there are times in your life when you must get the rest and relaxation which is so important in funding a strong nervous system. Drink plenty of water to flush out a system that can be over-high in natural salts.

Libra with Scorpio Ascendant

There is some tendency for you to be far more deep than the average Libran would appear to be, and for this reason it is crucial that you lighten up from time to time. Every person with a Scorpio quality needs to remember that there is a happy and carefree side to all events, and your Libran quality should allow you to bear this in mind. Sometimes you try to do too many things at the same time. This is fine if you take the casual overview of Libra, but less sensible when you insist on picking the last bone out of every potential, as is much more the case for Scorpio.

When worries come along, as they sometimes will, be able to listen to what your friends have to say and also realise that they are more than willing to work on your behalf, if only because you are so loyal to them. You do have a quality of self-deception, but this should not get in the way too much if you combine the instinctive actions of Libra with the deep intuition of your Scorpio component.

Probably the most important factor of this combination is your ability to succeed in a financial sense. You make a good manager, but not of the authoritarian sort. Jobs in the media or where you are expected to make up your mind quickly would suit you because there is always an underpinning of practical sense that rarely lets you down.

Libra with Sagittarius Ascendant

A very happy combination this, with a great desire for life in all its forms and a need to push forward the bounds of the possible in a way that few other zodiac sign connections would do. You don't like the unpleasant or ugly in life and yet you are capable of dealing with both if you have to. Giving so much to humanity, you still manage to retain a degree of individuality that would surprise many, charm others, and please all.

On the reverse side of the same coin you might find that you are sometimes accused of being fickle, but this is only an expression of your need for change and variety, which is endemic to both these signs. True, you have more of a temper than would be the case for Libra when taken on its own, but such incidents would see you up and down in a flash, and it is almost impossible for you to bear a grudge of any sort. Routines get on your nerves and you are far happier when you can please yourself and get ahead at your own pace, which is quite fast.

As a lover you can make a big impression and most of you will not go short of affection in the early days, before you choose to commit yourself. Once you do, there is always a chance of romantic problems, but these are less likely when you have chosen carefully in the first place.

Libra with Capricorn Ascendant

It is a fact that Libra is the most patient of the Air signs, though like the others it needs to get things done fairly quickly. Capricorn, on the other hand, will work long and hard to achieve its objectives and will not be thwarted in the end. As a result this is a quite powerful sign combination and one that should lead to ultimate success.

Capricorn is often accused of taking itself too seriously and yet it has an ironic and really very funny sense of humour which only its chief confidants recognise. Libra is lighthearted, always willing to have fun and quite anxious to please. When these two basic types come together in their best forms, you might find yourself to be one of the most well- balanced people around. Certainly you know what you want, but you don't have to use a bulldozer in order to get it.

Active and enthusiastic when something really takes your fancy, you might also turn out to be one of the very best lovers of them all. The reason for this is that you have the depth of Capricorn but the lighter and more directly affectionate qualities of the Scales. What you want from life in a personal sense, you eventually tend to get, but you don't care too much if this takes you a while. Few people could deny that you are a faithful friend, a happy sort and a deeply magnetic personality.

Libra with Aquarius Ascendant

Stand by for a truly interesting and very inspiring combination here, but one that is sometimes rather difficult to fathom, even for the sort of people who believe themselves to be very perceptive. The reason for this could be that any situation has to be essentially fixed and constant in order to get a handle on it, and this is certainly not the case for the Aquarian–Libran type. The fact is that both these signs are Air signs, and to a certain extent as unpredictable as the wind itself.

To most people you seem to be original, frank, free and very outspoken. Not everything you do makes sense to others, and if you were alive during the hippy era, it is likely that you went around with flowers in your hair, for you are a free-thinking idealist at heart. With age you mature somewhat, but never too much, because you will always see the strange, the comical and the original in life. This is what keeps you young and is one of the factors that makes you so very attractive to members of the opposite sex. Many people will want to 'adopt' you, and you are at your very best when in company.

Much of your effort is expounded on others and yet, unless you discipline yourself a good deal, personal relationships of the romantic sort can bring certain difficulties. Careful planning is necessary.

Libra with Pisces Ascendant

An Air and Water combination, you are not easy to understand and have depths that show at times, surprising those people who thought they already knew what you were. You will always keep people guessing and are just as likely to hitchhike around Europe as you are to hold down a steady job, both of which you would undertake with the same degree of commitment and success. Usually young at heart, but always carrying the potential for an old head on young shoulders, you are something of a paradox and not at all easy for totally 'straight' types to understand. But you always make an impression and tend to be very attractive to members of the opposite sex.

In matters of health you do have to be a little careful because you dissipate much nervous energy and can sometimes be inclined to push yourself too hard, at least in a mental sense. Frequent periods of rest and meditation will do you the world of good and should improve your level of wisdom, which tends to be fairly high already. Much of your effort in life is expounded on behalf of humanity as a whole, for you care deeply, love totally and always give of your best. Whatever your faults and failings might be, you are one of the most popular people around.

Libra with Aries Ascendant

Libra has the tendency to bring out the best in any zodiac sign, and this is no exception when it comes together with Aries. You may, in fact, be the most comfortable of all Aries types, simply because Libra tempers some of your more assertive qualities and gives you the chance to balance out opposing forces, both inside yourself and in the world outside. You are fun to be with and make the staunchest friend possible. Although you are generally affable, few people would try to put one over on you because they would quickly come to know how far you are willing to go before you let forth a string of invective that would shock those who previously underestimated your basic Aries traits.

Home and family are very dear to you, but you are more tolerant than some Aries types are inclined to be and you have a youthful zest for life that should stay with you no matter what age you manage to achieve. There is always something interesting to do and your mind is a constant stream of possibilities. This makes you very creative and you may also demonstrate a desire to look good at all times. You may not always be quite as confident as you appear to be, but few would guess the fact.

Libra with Taurus Ascendant

A fortunate combination in many ways, this is a double-Venus rulership, since both Taurus and Libra are heavily reliant on the planet of love. You are social, amiable and a natural diplomat, anxious to please and ready to care for just about anyone who shows interest in you. You hate disorder, which means that there is a place for everything and everything in its place. This can throw up the odd paradox however, since being half Libran you cannot always work out where that place ought to be! You deal with life in a humorous way and are quite capable of seeing the absurd in yourself, as well as in others. Your heart is no bigger than that of the quite typical Taurean, but it sits rather closer to the surface and so others recognise it more.

On those occasions when you know you are standing on firm ground you can show great confidence, even if you have to be ready to change some of your opinions at the drop of a hat. When this happens you can be quite at odds with yourself, because Taurus doesn't take very many U-turns, whereas Libra does. Don't expect to know yourself too well, and keep looking for the funny side of things, because it is within humour that you forge the sort of life that suits you best.

Libra with Gemini Ascendant

What a happy-go-lucky soul you are and how popular you tend to be with those around you. Libra is, like Gemini, an Air sign and this means that you are the communicator par excellence, even by Gemini standards. It can sometimes be difficult for you to make up your mind about things because Libra does not exactly aid this process, and especially not when it is allied to Mercurial Gemini. Frequent periods of deep thought are necessary, and meditation would do you a great deal of good. All the same, although you might sometimes be rather unsure of yourself, you are rarely without a certain balance. Clean and tidy surroundings suit you the best, though this is far from easy to achieve because you are invariably dashing off to some place or other, so you really need someone to sort things out in your absence.

The most important fact of all is that you are much loved by your friends, of which there are likely to be very many. Because you are so willing to help them out, in return they are usually there when it matters and they would probably go to almost any length on your behalf. You exhibit a fine sense of justice and will usually back those in trouble. Charities tend to be attractive to you and you do much on behalf of those who live on the fringes of society or people who are truly alone.

Libra with Cancer Ascendant

What an absolutely pleasant and approachable sort of person you are, and how much you have to offer. Like most people associated with the sign of Cancer you give yourself freely to the world, and will always be on hand if anyone is in trouble or needs the special touch you can bring to almost any problem. Behaving in this way is the biggest part of what you are and so people come to rely on you very heavily. Like Libra you can see both sides of any coin and you exhibit the Libran tendency to jump about from one foot to the other when it is necessary to make decisions relating to your own life. This is not usually the case when you are dealing with others however, because the cooler and more detached qualities of Cancer will show through in these circumstances.

It would be fair to say that you do not deal with routines as well as Cancer alone might do and you need a degree of variety in your life, which in your case often comes in the form of travel, which can be distant and of long duration. It isn't unusual for people who have this zodiac combination to end up living abroad, though even this does little to prevent you from getting itchy feet from time to time. In romance you show an original quality that keeps the relationship young and working very well.

Libra with Leo Ascendant

Libra brings slightly more flexibility to the fixed quality of the Leo nature. On the whole you do not represent a picture that is so much different from other versions of the Lion, though you find more time to smile, enjoy changing your mind a great deal more and have a greater number of casual friends. Few would find you proud or haughty and you retain the common touch that can be so important when it comes to getting on in life generally. At work you like to do something that brings variety, and would probably soon tire of doing the same task over and over again. Many of you are teachers, for you have patience, allied to a stubborn core. This can be an indispensable combination on occasions and is part of the reason for the material success that many folk with this combination of signs achieve.

It isn't often that you get down in the dumps, after all there is generally something more important around the next corner, and you love the cut and thrust of everyday life. You always manage to stay young at heart, no matter what your age might be, and you revel in the company of interesting and stimulating types. Maybe you should try harder to concentrate on one thing at once and also strive to retain a serious opinion for more than ten minutes at a time. However, Leo helps to control your flighty tendencies.

Libra with Virgo Ascendant

Libra has the ability to lighten almost any load, and it is particularly good at doing so when it is brought together with the much more repressed sign of Virgo. To the world at large you seem relaxed, happy and able to cope with most of the pressures that life places upon you. Not only do you deal with your own life in a bright and breezy manner but you are usually on hand to help others out of any dilemma that they might make for themselves. With excellent powers of communication, you leave the world at large in no doubt whatsoever concerning both your opinions and your wishes. It is in the talking stakes that you really excel because Virgo brings the silver tongue of Mercury and Libra adds the Air-sign desire to be in constant touch with the world outside your door.

You like to have a good time and can often be found in the company of interesting and stimulating people, who have the ability to bring out the very best in your bright and sparkling personality. Underneath however, there is still much of the worrying Virgoan to be found and this means that you have to learn to relax inside as well as appearing to do so externally. In fact you are much more complex than most people would realise, and definitely would not be suited to a life that allowed you too much time to think about yourself.

THE MOON AND THE PART IT PLAYS IN YOUR LIFE

In astrology the Moon is probably the single most important heavenly body after the Sun. Its unique position, as partner to the Earth on its journey around the solar system, means that the Moon appears to pass through the signs of the zodiac extremely quickly. The zodiac position of the Moon at the time of your birth plays a great part in personal character and is especially significant in the build-up of your emotional nature.

Your Own Moon Sign

Discovering the position of the Moon at the time of your birth has always been notoriously difficult because tracking the complex zodiac positions of the Moon is not easy. This process has been reduced to three simple stages with our Lunar Tables. A breakdown of the Moon's zodiac positions can be found from page 35 onwards, so that once you know what your Moon Sign is, you can see what part this plays in the overall build-up of your personal character.

If you follow the instructions on the next page you will soon be able to work out exactly what zodiac sign the Moon occupied on the day that you were born and you can then go on to compare the reading for this position with those of your Sun sign and your Ascendant. It is partly the comparison between these three important positions that goes towards making you the unique individual you are.

HOW TO DISCOVER YOUR MOON SIGN

This is a three-stage process. You may need a pen and a piece of paper but if you follow the instructions below the process should only take a minute or so.

STAGE 1 First of all you need to know the Moon Age at the time of your birth. If you look at Moon Table 1, on page 33, you will find all the years between 1916 and 2014 down the left side. Find the year of your birth and then trace across to the right to the month of your birth. Where the two intersect you will find a number. This is the date of the New Moon in the month that you were born. You now need to count forward the number of days between the New Moon and your own birthday. For example, if the New Moon in the month of your birth was shown as being the 6th and you were born on the 20th, your Moon Age Day would be 14. If the New Moon in the month of your birth came after your birthday, you need to count forward from the New Moon in the previous month. Whatever the result, jot this number down so that you do not forget it.

STAGE 2 Take a look at Moon Table 2 on page 34. Down the left hand column look for the date of your birth. Now trace across to the month of your birth. Where the two meet you will find a letter. Copy this letter down alongside your Moon Age Day.

STAGE 3 Moon Table 3 on page 34 will supply you with the zodiac sign the Moon occupied on the day of your birth. Look for your Moon Age Day down the left hand column and then for the letter you found in Stage 2. Where the two converge you will find a zodiac sign and this is the sign occupied by the Moon on the day that you were born.

Your Zodiac Moon Sign Explained

You will find a profile of all zodiac Moon Signs on pages 35 to 38, showing in yet another way how astrology helps to make you into the individual that you are. In each daily entry of the Astral Diary you can find the zodiac position of the Moon for every day of the year. This also allows you to discover your lunar birthdays. Since the Moon passes through all the signs of the zodiac in about a month, you can expect something like twelve lunar birthdays each year. At these times you are likely to be emotionally steady and able to make the sort of decisions that have real, lasting value.

MOON TABLE 1

YEAR	AUG	SEP	OCT	YEAR	AUG	SEP	OCT	YEAR	AUG	SEP	OCT
1916	29	27	27	1949	24	23	21	1982	19	17	17
1917	17	15	15	1950	13	12	11	1983	8	7	6
1918	6	4	4	1951	2	1	1/30	1984	26	25	24
1919	25	23	23	1952	20	19	18	1985	16	14	14
1920	14	12	12	1953	9	8	8	1986	5	4	3
1921	3	2	1/30	1954	28	27	26	1987	24	23	22
1922	22	21	20	1955	17	16	15	1988	12	11	10
1923	12	10	10	1956	6	4	4	1989	1/31	29	29
1924	30	28	28	1957	25	23	23	1990	20	19	18
1925	19	18	17	1958	15	13	12	1991	9	8	8
1926	8	7	6	1959	4	3	2/31	1992	28	26	25
1927	27	25	25	1960	22	21	20	1993	17	16	15
1928	16	14	14	1961	11	10	9	1994	7	5	5
1929	5	3	2	1962	30	28	28	1995	26	24	24
1930	24	22	20	1963	19	17	17	1996	14	13	11
1931	13	12	11	1964	7	6	5	1997	3	2	2/31
1932	2/31	30	29	1965	26	25	24	1998	22	20	20
1933	21	19	19	1966	16	14	14	1999	11	10	8
1934	10	9	8	1967	5	4	3	2000	29	27	27
1935	29	27	27	1968	24	23	22	2001	19	17	17
1936	17	15	15	1969	12	11	10	2002	8	6	6
1937	6	4	4	1970	2	1	1/30	2003	27	26	25
1938	25	23	23	1971	20	19	19	2004	14	13	12
1939	15	13	12	1972	9	8	8	2005	4	3	2
1940	4	2	1/30	1973	28	27	26	2006	23	22	21
1941	22	21	20	1974	17	16	15	2007	13	12	11
1942	12	10	10	1975	7	5	5	2008	1/31	30	29
1943	1/30	29	29	1976	25	23	23	2009	20	19	18
1944	18	17	17	1977	14	13	12	2010	10	8	8
1945	8	6	6	1978	4	2	2/31	2011	29	27	27
1946	26	25	24	1979	22	21	20	2012	17	16	15
1947	16	14	14	1980	11	10	9	2013	6	4	4
1948	5	3	2	1981	29	28	27	2014	24	23	22

TABLE 2

DAY	SEP	OCT
1	X	a
2	X	a
3	X	a
4	Y	b
5	Y	b
6	Y	b
7	Y	b
8	Y	b
9	Y	b
10	Y	b
11	Y	b
12	Y	b
13	Y	b
14	Z	d
15	Z	d
16	Z	d
17	Z	d
18	Z	d
19	Z	d
20	Z	d
21	Z	d
22	Z	d
23	Z	d
24	a	e
25	a	e
26	a	e
27	a	e
28	a	e
29	a	e
30	a	e
31	–	e

MOON TABLE 3

M/D	X	Y	Z	a	b	d	e
0	VI	VI	LI	LI	LI	LI	SC
1	VI	LI	LI	LI	LI	SC	SC
2	LI	LI	LI	LI	SC	SC	SC
3	LI	LI	SC	SC	SC	SC	SA
4	LI	SC	SC	SC	SA	SA	SA
5	SC	SC	SC	SA	SA	SA	CP
6	SC	SA	SA	SA	CP	CP	CP
7	SA	SA	SA	SA	CP	CP	AQ
8	SA	SA	CP	CP	CP	CP	AQ
9	SA	CP	CP	CP	AQ	AQ	AQ
10	CP	CP	CP	AQ	AQ	AQ	PI
11	CP	AQ	AQ	AQ	PI	PI	PI
12	AQ	AQ	AQ	PI	PI	PI	AR
13	AQ	AQ	PI	PI	AR	PI	AR
14	PI	PI	PI	AR	AR	AR	TA
15	PI	PI	PI	AR	AR	AR	TA
16	PI	AR	AR	AR	AR	TA	TA
17	AR	AR	AR	AR	TA	TA	GE
18	AR	AR	AR	TA	TA	GE	GE
19	AR	TA	TA	TA	TA	GE	GE
20	TA	TA	TA	GE	GE	GE	CA
21	TA	GE	GE	GE	GE	CA	CA
22	GE	GE	GE	GE	CA	CA	CA
23	GE	GE	GE	CA	CA	CA	LE
24	GE	CA	CA	CA	CA	LE	LE
25	CA	CA	CA	CA	LE	LE	LE
26	CA	LE	LE	LE	LE	VI	VI
27	LE	LE	LE	LE	VI	VI	VI
28	LE	LE	LE	VI	VI	VI	LI
29	LE	VI	VI	VI	VI	LI	LI

AR = Aries, TA = Taurus, GE = Gemini, CA = Cancer, LE = Leo, VI = Virgo, LI = Libra, SC = Scorpio, SA = Sagittarius, CP = Capricorn, AQ = Aquarius, PI = Pisces

MOON SIGNS

Moon in Aries

You have a strong imagination, courage, determination and a desire to do things in your own way and forge your own path through life.

Originality is a key attribute; you are seldom stuck for ideas although your mind is changeable and you could take the time to focus on individual tasks. Often quick-tempered, you take orders from few people and live life at a fast pace. Avoid health problems by taking regular time out for rest and relaxation.

Emotionally, it is important that you talk to those you are closest to and work out your true feelings. Once you discover that people are there to help, there is less necessity for you to do everything yourself.

Moon in Taurus

The Moon in Taurus gives you a courteous and friendly manner, which means you are likely to have many friends.

The good things in life mean a lot to you, as Taurus is an Earth sign that delights in experiences which please the senses. Hence you are probably a lover of good food and drink, which may in turn mean you need to keep an eye on the bathroom scales, especially as looking good is also important to you.

Emotionally you are fairly stable and you stick by your own standards. Taureans do not respond well to change. Intuition also plays an important part in your life.

Moon in Gemini

You have a warm-hearted character, sympathetic and eager to help others. At times reserved, you can also be articulate and chatty: this is part of the paradox of Gemini, which always brings duplicity to the nature. You are interested in current affairs, have a good intellect, and are good company and likely to have many friends. Most of your friends have a high opinion of you and would be ready to defend you should the need arise. However, this is usually unnecessary, as you are quite capable of defending yourself in any verbal confrontation.

Travel is important to your inquisitive mind and you find intellectual stimulus in mixing with people from different cultures. You also gain much from reading, writing and the arts but you do need plenty of rest and relaxation in order to avoid fatigue.

Moon in Cancer

The Moon in Cancer at the time of birth is a fortunate position as Cancer is the Moon's natural home. This means that the qualities of compassion and understanding given by the Moon are especially enhanced in your nature, and you are friendly and sociable and cope well with emotional pressures. You cherish home and family life, and happily do the domestic tasks. Your surroundings are important to you and you hate squalor and filth. You are likely to have a love of music and poetry.

Your basic character, although at times changeable like the Moon itself, depends on symmetry. You aim to make your surroundings comfortable and harmonious, for yourself and those close to you.

Moon in Leo

The best qualities of the Moon and Leo come together to make you warm-hearted, fair, ambitious and self-confident. With good organisational abilities, you invariably rise to a position of responsibility in your chosen career. This is fortunate as you don't enjoy being an 'also-ran' and would rather be an important part of a small organisation than a menial in a large one.

You should be lucky in love, and happy, provided you put in the effort to make a comfortable home for yourself and those close to you. It is likely that you will have a love of pleasure, sport, music and literature. Life brings you many rewards, most of them as a direct result of your own efforts, although you may be luckier than average and ready to make the best of any situation.

Moon in Virgo

You are endowed with good mental abilities and a keen receptive memory, but you are never ostentatious or pretentious. Naturally quite reserved, you still have many friends, especially of the opposite sex. Marital relationships must be discussed carefully and worked at so that they remain harmonious, as personal attachments can be a problem if you do not give them your full attention.

Talented and persevering, you possess artistic qualities and are a good homemaker. Earning your honours through genuine merit, you work long and hard towards your objectives but show little pride in your achievements. Many short journeys will be undertaken in your life.

Moon in Libra

With the Moon in Libra you are naturally popular and make friends easily. People like you, probably more than you realise, you bring fun to a party and are a natural diplomat. For all its good points, Libra is not the most stable of astrological signs and, as a result, your emotions can be a little unstable too. Therefore, although the Moon in Libra is said to be good for love and marriage, your Sun sign and Rising sign will have an important effect on your emotional and loving qualities.

You must remember to relate to others in your decision-making. Co-operation is crucial because Libra represents the 'balance' of life that can only be achieved through harmonious relationships. Conformity is not easy for you because Libra, an Air sign, likes its independence.

Moon in Scorpio

Some people might call you pushy. In fact, all you really want to do is to live life to the full and protect yourself and your family from the pressures of life. Take care to avoid giving the impression of being sarcastic or impulsive and use your energies wisely and constructively.

You have great courage and you invariably achieve your goals by force of personality and sheer effort. You are fond of mystery and are good at predicting the outcome of situations and events. Travel experiences can be beneficial to you.

You may experience problems if you do not take ti[illegible]e to examine your motives in a relationship, and also if you allow jealousy, always a feature of Scorpio, to cloud your judgement.

Moon in Sagittarius

T[illegible]vidual with h[illegible]be intrinsic as [illegible]ave a need fo[illegible]ring your ad[illegible]ou know you[illegible]tuition. [illegible] make an idea[illegible]ing and do n[illegible]

I[illegible] faced with stupidity or decep[illegible] you are just as quick to forgive and forget. Emot[illegible]nally, there are times when your heart rules your head.

Moon Sign
Stage 1
New moon in Oct 1948
was 2nd Oct.
Sept 3- to Oct 1" = 28 days
Stage 2 = a
Stage 3 28, a
Moon Age Day
= Virgo
∴ Moon in Virgo

Moon in Capricorn

The Moon in Capricorn makes you popular and likely to come into the public eye in some way. The watery Moon is not entirely comfortable in the Earth sign of Capricorn and this may lead to some difficulties in the early years of life. An initial lack of creative ability and indecision must be overcome before the true qualities of patience and perseverance inherent in Capricorn can show through.

You have good administrative ability and are a capable worker, and if you are careful you can accumulate wealth. But you must be cautious and take professional advice in partnerships, as you are open to deception. You may be interested in social or welfare work, which suit your organisational skills and sympathy for others.

Moon in Aquarius

The Moon in Aquarius makes you an active and agreeable person with a friendly, easy-going nature. Sympathetic to the needs of others, you flourish in a laid-back atmosphere. You are broad-minded, fair and open to suggestion, although sometimes you have an unconventional quality which others can find hard to understand.

You are interested in the strange and curious, and in old articles and places. You enjoy trips to these places and gain much from them. Political, scientific and educational work interests you and you might choose a career in science or technology.

Money-wise, you make gains through innovation and concentration and Lunar Aquarians often tackle more than one job at a time. In love you are kind and honest.

Moon in Pisces

You have a kind, sympathetic nature, somewhat retiring at times, but you always take account of others' feelings and help when you can.

Personal relationships may be problematic, but as life goes on you can learn from your experiences and develop a better understanding of yourself and the world around you.

You have a fondness for travel, appreciate beauty and harmony and hate disorder and strife. You may be fond of literature and would make a good writer or speaker yourself. You have a creative imagination and may come across as an incurable romantic. You have strong intuition, maybe bordering on a mediumistic quality, which sets you apart from the mass. You may not be rich in cash terms, but your personal gifts are worth more than gold.

LIBRA IN LOVE

Discover how compatible you are with people from the same and other signs of the zodiac. Five stars equals a match made in heaven!

Libra meets Libra Sept, Oct

This is a potentially successful match because Librans are extremely likeable people, and so it stands to reason that two Librans together will be twice as pleasant and twice as much fun. However, Librans can also be indecisive and need an anchor from which to find practical and financial success, and obviously one Libran won't provide this for another. Librans can be flighty in a romantic sense, so both parties will need to develop a steadfast approach for a long-term relationship. Star rating: ****

Libra meets Scorpio Oct. Nov.

Many astrologers have reservations about this match because, on the surface, the signs are so different. However, this couple may find fulfilment because these differences mean that their respective needs are met. Scorpio needs a partner to lighten the load which won't daunt Libra, while Libra looks for a steadfast quality which it doesn't possess, but Scorpio can supply naturally. Financial success is possible because they both have good ideas and back them up with hard work and determination. All in all, a promising outlook. Star rating: ****

Libra meets Sagittarius Nov, Dec,

Libra and Sagittarius are both adaptable signs who get on well with most people, but this promising outlook often does not follow through because each brings out the flighty side of the other. This combination is great for a fling, but when the romance is over someone needs to see to the practical side of life. Both signs are well meaning, pleasant and kind, but are either of them constant enough to build a life together? In at least some of the cases, the answer would be no. Star rating: ***

Libra meets Capricorn Dec. Jan.

Libra and Capricorn rub each other up the wrong way because their attitudes to life are so different, and although both are capable of doing something about this, in reality they probably won't. Capricorn is steady, determined and solid, while Libra is bright but sometimes superficial and not entirely reliable. They usually lack the instant spark needed to get them together in the first place, so when it does happen it is often because one of the partners is not typical of their sign. Star rating: **

Libra meets Aquarius Jan. Feb.

One of the best combinations imaginable, partly because both are Air signs and so share a common meeting point. But perhaps the more crucial factor is that both signs respect each other. Aquarius loves life and originality, and is quite intellectual. Libra is similar, but more balanced and rather less eccentric. A visit to this couple's house would be entertaining and full of zany wit, activity and excitement. Both are keen to travel and may prefer to 'find themselves' before taking on too many domestic responsibilities. Star rating: *****

Libra meets Pisces Feb. Mar.

Libra and Pisces can be extremely fond of each other, even deeply in love, but this alone isn't a stable foundation for long-term success. Pisces is extremely deep and doesn't even know itself very well. Libra may initially find this intriguing but will eventually feel frustrated at being unable to understand the Piscean's emotional and personal feelings. Pisces can be jealous and may find Libra's flightiness difficult, which Libra can't stand. They are great friends and they may make it to the romantic stakes, but when they get there a lot of effort will be necessary. Star rating: ***

Libra meets Aries Mar, April

These are zodiac opposites which means a make-or-break situation. The match will either be a great success or a dismal failure. Why? Well, Aries finds it difficult to understand the flighty Air-sign tendencies of Libra, whilst the natural balance of Libra contradicts the unorthodox Arian methods. Any flexibility will come from Libra, which may mean that things work out for a while, but Libra only has so much patience and it may eventually run out. In the end, Aries may be just too bossy for an independent but sensitive sign like Libra. Star rating: **

Libra meets Taurus April, May

A happy life is important to both these signs and, as they are both ruled by Venus, they share a common understanding, even though they display themselves so differently. Taurus is quieter than Libra, but can be decisive, and that's what counts. Libra is interested in absolutely everything, an infectious quality when seen through Taurean eyes. The slightly flighty qualities of Libra may lead to jealousy from the Bull. Not an argumentative relationship and one that often works well. There could be many changes of address for this pair. Star rating: ****

Libra meets Gemini May, June

One of the best possible zodiac combinations. Libra and Gemini are both Air signs, which leads to a meeting of minds. Both signs simply love to have a good time, although Libra is the tidiest and less forgetful. Gemini's capricious nature won't bother Libra, who acts as a stabilising influence. Life should generally run smoothly, and any rows are likely to be short and sharp. Both parties genuinely like each other, which is of paramount importance in a relationship and, ultimately, there isn't a better reason for being or staying together. Star rating: *****

Libra meets Cancer June, July

Almost anyone can get on with Libra, which is one of the most adaptable signs of them all. But being adaptable does not always lead to fulfilment and a successful match here will require a quiet Libran and a slightly more progressive Cancerian than the norm. Both signs are pleasant and polite, and like domestic order, but Libra may find Cancer too emotional and perhaps lacking in vibrancy, while Libra, on the other hand, may be a little too flighty for steady Cancer. Star rating: ***

Libra meets Leo July, Aug.

The biggest drawback here is likely to be in the issue of commitment. Leo knows everything about constancy and faithfulness, a lesson which, sadly, Libra needs to learn. Librans are easy-going and diplomatic, qualities which are useful when Leo is on the war-path. This couple should be compatible on a personal level and any problems tend to relate to the different way in which these signs deal with outside factors. With good will and an open mind, it can work out well enough. Star rating: ***

Libra meets Virgo Aug. Sept.

There have been some rare occasions when this match has found great success, but usually the darker and more inward-looking Virgoan depresses the naturally gregarious Libran. Libra appears self-confident, but is not so beneath the surface, and needs encouragement to develop inner confidence, which may not come from Virgo. Constancy can be a problem for Libra, who also tires easily and may find Virgo dull. A lighter, less serious approach to life from Virgo is needed to make this work. Star rating: **

VENUS: THE PLANET OF LOVE

If you look up at the sky around sunset or sunrise you will often see Venus in close attendance to the Sun. It is arguably one of the most beautiful sights of all and there is little wonder that historically it became associated with the goddess of love. But although Venus does play an important part in the way you view love and in the way others see you romantically, this is only one of the spheres of influence that it enjoys in your overall character.

Venus has a part to play in the more cultured side of your life and has much to do with your appreciation of art, literature, music and general creativity. Even the way you look is responsive to the part of the zodiac that Venus occupied at the start of your life, though this fact is also down to your Sun sign and Ascending sign. If, at the time you were born, Venus occupied one of the more gregarious zodiac signs, you will be more likely to wear your heart on your sleeve, as well as to be more attracted to entertainment, social gatherings and good company. If on the other hand Venus occupied a quiet zodiac sign at the time of your birth, you would tend to be more retiring and less willing to shine in public situations.

It's good to know what part the planet Venus plays in your life for it can have a great bearing on the way you appear to the rest of the world and since we all have to mix with others, you can learn to make the very best of what Venus has to offer you.

One of the great complications in the past has always been trying to establish exactly what zodiac position Venus enjoyed when you were born because the planet is notoriously difficult to track. However, we have solved that problem by creating a table that is exclusive to your Sun sign, which you will find on the following page.

Establishing your Venus sign could not be easier. Just look up the year of your birth on the next page and you will see a sign of the zodiac. This was the sign that Venus occupied in the period covered by your sign in that year. If Venus occupied more than one sign during the period, this is indicated by the date on which the sign changed, and the name of the new sign. For instance, if you were born in 1950, Venus was in Virgo until the 4th October, after which time it was in Libra. If you were born before 4th October your Venus sign is Virgo, if you were born on or after 4th October, your Venus sign is Libra. Once you have established the position of Venus at the time of your birth, you can then look in the pages which follow to see how this has a bearing on your life as a whole.

1916 LEO / 8.10 VIRGO
1917 SCORPIO / 12.10 SAGITTARIUS
1918 VIRGO / 6.10 LIBRA
1919 SCORPIO / 12.10 SAGITTARIUS
1920 LIBRA / 30.9 SCORPIO
1921 LEO / 26.9 VIRGO / 21.10 LIBRA
1922 SCORPIO / 11.10 SAGITTARIUS
1923 LIBRA / 16.10 SCORPIO
1924 LEO / 8.10 VIRGO
1925 SCORPIO / 12.10 SAGITTARIUS
1926 VIRGO / 6.10 LIBRA
1927 VIRGO
1928 LIBRA / 29.9 SCORPIO
1929 LEO / 26.9 VIRGO / 20.10 LIBRA
1930 SCORPIO / 12.10 SAGITTARIUS
1931 LIBRA / 15.10 SCORPIO
1932 LEO / 7.10 VIRGO
1933 SCORPIO / 11.10 SAGITTARIUS
1934 VIRGO / 5.10 LIBRA
1935 VIRGO
1936 LIBRA / 28.9 SCORPIO
1937 LEO / 25.9 VIRGO / 20.10 LIBRA
1938 SCORPIO / 14.10 SAGITTARIUS
1939 LIBRA / 14.10 SCORPIO
1940 LEO / 7.10 VIRGO
1941 SCORPIO / 11.10 SAGITTARIUS
1942 VIRGO / 5.10 LIBRA
1943 VIRGO
1944 LIBRA / 28.9 SCORPIO
1945 LEO / 25.9 VIRGO / 19.10 LIBRA
1946 SCORPIO / 14.10 SAGITTARIUS
1947 LIBRA / 13.10 SCORPIO
1948 LEO / 7.10 VIRGO
1949 SCORPIO / 11.10 SAGITTARIUS
1950 VIRGO / 4.10 LIBRA
1951 VIRGO
1952 LIBRA / 27.9 SCORPIO
1953 VIRGO / 19.10 LIBRA
1954 SCORPIO / 16.10 SAGITTARIUS
1955 LIBRA / 12.10 SCORPIO
1956 LEO / 6.10 VIRGO
1957 SCORPIO / 10.10 SAGITTARIUS
1958 VIRGO / 4.10 LIBRA
1959 VIRGO / 28.9 LEO
1960 LIBRA / 27.9 SCORPIO
1961 VIRGO / 18.10 LIBRA
1962 SCORPIO / 16.10 SAGITTARIUS
1963 LIBRA / 12.10 SCORPIO
1964 LEO / 6.10 VIRGO
1965 SCORPIO / 9.10 SAGITTARIUS
1966 VIRGO / 4.10 LIBRA
1967 VIRGO / 3.10 LEO
1968 LIBRA / 26.9 SCORPIO
1969 VIRGO / 17.10 LIBRA
1970 SCORPIO / 19.10 SAGITTARIUS
1971 LIBRA / 11.10 SCORPIO
1972 LEO / 6.10 VIRGO
1973 SCORPIO / 9.10 SAGITTARIUS
1974 VIRGO / 3.10 LIBRA
1975 VIRGO / 5.10 LEO
1976 LIBRA / 26.9 SCORPIO
1977 VIRGO / 17.10 LIBRA
1978 SCORPIO / 19.10 SAGITTARIUS
1979 LIBRA / 11.10 SCORPIO
1980 LEO / 5.10 VIRGO
1981 SCORPIO / 9.10 SAGITTARIUS
1982 VIRGO / 3.10 LIBRA
1983 VIRGO / 7.10 LEO
1984 LIBRA / 25.9 SCORPIO
1985 VIRGO / 16.10 LIBRA
1986 SCORPIO
1987 LIBRA / 10.10 SCORPIO
1988 LEO / 5.10 VIRGO
1989 SCORPIO / 8.10 SAGITTARIUS
1990 VIRGO / 2.10 LIBRA
1991 VIRGO / 8.10 LEO
1992 LIBRA / 25.9 SCORPIO
1993 VIRGO / 16.10 LIBRA
1994 SCORPIO
1995 LIBRA / 10.10 SCORPIO
1996 LEO / 5.10 VIRGO
1997 SCORPIO / 8.10 SAGITTARIUS
1998 VIRGO / 2.10 LIBRA
1999 VIRGO / 9.10 LEO
2000 LIBRA / 25.9 SCORPIO
2001 LEO / 5.10 VIRGO
2002 SCORPIO / 8.10 SAGITTARIUS
2003 LIBRA / 10.10 SCORPIO
2004 LEO / 5.10 VIRGO
2005 SCORPIO / 8.10 SAGITTARIUS
2006 VIRGO / 2.10 LIBRA
2007 VIRGO / 9.10 LEO
2008 LIBRA / 25.9 SCORPIO
2009 LEO / 5.10 VIRGO
2010 SCORPIO / 8.10 SAGITTARIUS
2011 LIBRA / 10.10 SCORPIO
2012 LEO / 5.10 VIRGO
2013 SCORPIO / 8.10 SAGITTARIUS
2014 VIRGO / 2.10 LIBRA

VENUS THROUGH THE ZODIAC SIGNS

Venus in Aries

Amongst other things, the position of Venus in Aries indicates a fondness for travel, music and all creative pursuits. Your nature tends to be affectionate and you would try not to create confusion or difficulty for others if it could be avoided. Many people with this planetary position have a great love of the theatre, and mental stimulation is of the greatest importance. Early romantic attachments are common with Venus in Aries, so it is very important to establish a genuine sense of romantic continuity. Early marriage is not recommended, especially if it is based on sympathy. You may give your heart a little too readily on occasions.

Venus in Taurus

You are capable of very deep feelings and your emotions tend to last for a very long time. This makes you a trusting partner and lover, whose constancy is second to none. In life you are precise and careful and always try to do things the right way. Although this means an ordered life, which you are comfortable with, it can also lead you to be rather too fussy for your own good. Despite your pleasant nature, you are very fixed in your opinions and quite able to speak your mind. Others are attracted to you and historical astrologers always quoted this position of Venus as being very fortunate in terms of marriage. However, if you find yourself involved in a failed relationship, it could take you a long time to trust again.

Venus in Gemini

As with all associations related to Gemini, you tend to be quite versatile, anxious for change and intelligent in your dealings with the world at large. You may gain money from more than one source but you are equally good at spending it. There is an inference here that you are a good communicator, via either the written or the spoken word, and you love to be in the company of interesting people. Always on the look-out for culture, you may also be very fond of music, and love to indulge the curious and cultured side of your nature. In romance you tend to have more than one relationship and could find yourself associated with someone who has previously been a friend or even a distant relative.

Venus in Cancer

You often stay close to home because you are very fond of family and enjoy many of your most treasured moments when you are with those you love. Being naturally sympathetic, you will always do anything you can to support those around you, even people you hardly know at all. This charitable side of your nature is your most noticeable trait and is one of the reasons why others are naturally so fond of you. Being receptive and in some cases even psychic, you can see through to the soul of most of those with whom you come into contact. You may not commence too many romantic attachments but when you do give your heart, it tends to be unconditionally.

Venus in Leo

It must become quickly obvious to almost anyone you meet that you are kind, sympathetic and yet determined enough to stand up for anyone or anything that is truly important to you. Bright and sunny, you warm the world with your natural enthusiasm and would rarely do anything to hurt those around you, or at least not intentionally. In romance you are ardent and sincere, though some may find your style just a little overpowering. Gains come through your contacts with other people and this could be especially true with regard to romance, for love and money often come hand in hand for those who were born with Venus in Leo. People claim to understand you, though you are more complex than you seem.

Venus in Virgo

Your nature could well be fairly quiet no matter what your Sun sign might be, though this fact often manifests itself as an inner peace and would not prevent you from being basically sociable. Some delays and even the odd disappointment in love cannot be ruled out with this planetary position, though it's a fact that you will usually find the happiness you look for in the end. Catapulting yourself into romantic entanglements that you know to be rather ill-advised is not sensible, and it would be better to wait before you committed yourself exclusively to any one person. It is the essence of your nature to serve the world at large and through doing so it is possible that you will attract money at some stage in your life.

Venus in Libra

Venus is very comfortable in Libra and bestows upon those people who have this planetary position a particular sort of kindness that is easy to recognise. This is a very good position for all sorts of friendships and also for romantic attachments that usually bring much joy into your life. Few individuals with Venus in Libra would avoid marriage and since you are capable of great depths of love, it is likely that you will find a contented personal life. You like to mix with people of integrity and intelligence but don't take kindly to scruffy surroundings or work that means getting your hands too dirty. Careful speculation, good business dealings and money through marriage all seem fairly likely.

Venus in Scorpio

You are quite open and tend to spend money quite freely, even on those occasions when you don't have very much. Although your intentions are always good, there are times when you get yourself in to the odd scrape and this can be particularly true when it comes to romance, which you may come to late or from a rather unexpected direction. Certainly you have the power to be happy and to make others contented on the way, but you find the odd stumbling block on your journey through life and it would seem that you have to work harder than those around you. As a result of this, you gain a much deeper understanding of the true value of personal happiness than many people ever do, and are likely to achieve true contentment in the end.

Venus in Sagittarius

You are light-hearted, cheerful and always able to see the funny side of any situation. These facts enhance your popularity, which is especially high with members of the opposite sex. You should never have to look too far to find romantic interest in your life, though it is just possible that you might be too willing to commit yourself before you are certain that the person in question is right for you. Part of the problem here extends to other areas of life too. The fact is that you like variety in everything and so can tire of situations that fail to offer it. All the same, if you choose wisely and learn to understand your restless side, then great happiness can be yours.

Venus in Capricorn

The most notable trait that comes from Venus in this position is that it makes you trustworthy and able to take on all sorts of responsibilities in life. People are instinctively fond of you and love you all the more because you are always ready to help those who are in any form of need. Social and business popularity can be yours and there is a magnetic quality to your nature that is particularly attractive in a romantic sense. Anyone who wants a partner for a lover, a spouse and a good friend too would almost certainly look in your direction. Constancy is the hallmark of your nature and unfaithfulness would go right against the grain. You might sometimes be a little too trusting.

Venus in Aquarius

This location of Venus offers a fondness for travel and a desire to try out something new at every possible opportunity. You are extremely easy to get along with and tend to have many friends from varied backgrounds, classes and inclinations. You like to live a distinct sort of life and gain a great deal from moving about, both in a career sense and with regard to your home. It is not out of the question that you could form a romantic attachment to someone who comes from far away or be attracted to a person of a distinctly artistic and original nature. What you cannot stand is jealousy, for you have friends of both sexes and would want to keep things that way.

Venus in Pisces

The first thing people tend to notice about you is your wonderful, warm smile. Being very charitable by nature you will do anything to help others, even if you don't know them well. Much of your life may be spent sorting out situations for other people, but it is very important to feel that you are living for yourself too. In the main, you remain cheerful, and tend to be quite attractive to members of the opposite sex. Where romantic attachments are concerned, you could be drawn to people who are significantly older or younger than yourself or to someone with a unique career or point of view. It might be best for you to avoid marrying whilst you are still very young.

LIBRA:
2013 DIARY PAGES

October
2013

1 TUESDAY *Moon Age Day 27 Moon Sign Leo*

There is now a change of emphasis as far as your love life is concerned, and you may need to begin doing things in a slightly different way. Even in terms of friendship, variety proves to be the spice of life at this time. There are signs that any recent tendency to ill-health should be clearing up at this time.

2 WEDNESDAY *Moon Age Day 28 Moon Sign Virgo*

Venus can offer a boost to finances, though you will have to lend a hand. Keep your eyes open for bargains. This is also a favourable time for selling items you no longer need. Perhaps a rummage through the attic would help? No matter how you go about it, it's time to look for ways to improve your income.

3 THURSDAY *Moon Age Day 29 Moon Sign Virgo*

Some hopeful information may now come your way regarding your personal wishes. There is much to be said for putting to one side any matters you have been worrying about and pushing on towards a specific objective. Once again Venus comes to your aid in terms of love. Listen carefully to what people are really saying.

4 FRIDAY *Moon Age Day 0 Moon Sign Virgo*

Making your mind up instantly can be quite rewarding at the moment. This is really no time for standing around and thinking. Everything comes to you when you are decisive and willing to take the lead. Not everyone will want to follow, though the people who matter the most at present probably will.

00.35 new moon

5 SATURDAY *Moon Age Day 1 Moon Sign Libra*

The best of all worlds is possible today. The Sun is in your solar first house and the Moon is in your zodiac sign. All in all you can make today your own. Go for what you want in life and don't accept any excuses, particularly from yourself. You can capitalise on a real boost to your energy and a tremendous sense of urgency.

6 SUNDAY *Moon Age Day 2 Moon Sign Libra*

At the moment your generosity is to the fore. That's fine, as long as you can afford to lavish money and gifts on others. Where younger family members are concerned you may discover that a little more attention is worth any amount of material gifts. Be willing to confront one or two small fears now.

7 MONDAY *Moon Age Day 3 Moon Sign Scorpio*

Intimate relationships can now help you to increase your own sense of security, and enable you to feel closer to a particular individual than has been the case for quite some time. Monetary bonuses could also be within your grasp, perhaps coming as a result of efforts that you have put in previously.

8 TUESDAY *Moon Age Day 4 Moon Sign Scorpio*

The sort of information that you can gather via normal conversation could be worth its weight in gold. As a result, this is a day when you really need to pin back your ears and listen. The most mundane form of gossip carries messages that you can turn into a wealth of advantages in the weeks and months ahead.

9 WEDNESDAY *Moon Age Day 5 Moon Sign Sagittarius*

This is a day to enjoy the fruits of some of your past efforts. Even if you feel you are closer than ever to making an important breakthrough in your life, taking a rest would be no bad thing. Make the most of social invitations and any opportunities for love. The only thing to remember is to avoid provoking jealousy in others.

Jenie & I were thrilled to have first sighting of new moon at around 7.20pm as we went, plus Mo, to Elim College. We saw it again at interval, sinking fast in the west; gone at 9.40pm !

10 THURSDAY *Moon Age Day 6 Moon Sign Sagittarius*

You continue on a roll with all practical matters and should be able to make certain that you are making progress when it comes to work. This doesn't mean that you should slacken your pace. On the contrary, once you have the bit between your teeth you should be pushing onwards and upwards that much harder.

11 FRIDAY *Moon Age Day 7 Moon Sign Capricorn*

In the practical stakes you should once again be achieving plenty right now. If there is something you have wanted to do for a while, but you have shied away from it, now is the time. Prepare to persuade those you hold dearest to give you some useful and even exceptional assistance. 1st ¼ at 23.02

12 SATURDAY *Moon Age Day 8 Moon Sign Capricorn*

There are signs that personal indulgences could come well down your list of priorities today. The emphasis is on the side of your nature that is concerned with looking out for others. If possible, do an extra job right now, giving you time tomorrow to do what you please. Any confusion in relationships can soon be cleared up.

13 SUNDAY *Moon Age Day 9 Moon Sign Aquarius*

Today is an opportunity for you to impress others with both your knowledge and your resilience. Keep up your efforts to get through to difficult types, though not to the extent that you can't make any real practical progress. You can make this a Sunday to remember if you are willing to keep putting in the effort.

14 MONDAY *Moon Age Day 10 Moon Sign Aquarius*

You have it within you to impress the right sort of people at the beginning of this week. If you are a working Libran you can now afford to take on newer and more demanding responsibilities. Not only can these help you to pep up your professional life, they should offer the chance of some financial rewards.

15 TUESDAY *Moon Age Day 11 Moon Sign Pisces*

It pays to be fired up and ready for challenges at work. You can capitalise on a potentially enterprising and enlightening period, which could include tackling any current relationship problems. You would also be wise to take care over money matters. If deals look too good to be true, they probably are!

16 WEDNESDAY *Moon Age Day 12 Moon Sign Pisces*

Emotional issues and the way you view them could well dominate personal relationships at present, whereas practical matters should be taking centre stage. If you can, defuse issues before they take on any real importance and avoid getting involved in discussions you know could be contentious.

17 THURSDAY *Moon Age Day 13 Moon Sign Pisces*

Trends indicate you could be on a roll at present. Not only can you increase your popularity, you should also be able to use your silver-tongued eloquence to help you get you what you want from life. Nevertheless, you might still be pulled up in your tracks tomorrow, when the lunar low comes along.

18 FRIDAY *Moon Age Day 14 Moon Sign Aries*

If you enter this month's lunar low in a very positive frame of mind, you might not even have too much reason to notice its presence. Continue to go for what you want in life generally, though realise that when you shoot for the stars you might only reach the moon. It pays to shun as many rules and regulations as you can.

19 SATURDAY *Moon Age Day 15 Moon Sign Aries*

It would probably be a good idea to suspend a few of your efforts for today. The lunar low doesn't necessarily prevent you from getting ahead, though it might make the path somewhat harder to follow. Why not let those around you take the strain while you deliberately choose to take a short break.

20 SUNDAY *Moon Age Day 16 Moon Sign Taurus*

There is plenty of initiative available for professional developments under present trends. There's nothing wrong with allowing simple friendship to take something of a back seat at this stage of the week, especially if you are busy with other activities. Caution is the key when it comes to financial matters.

21 MONDAY ☿ *Moon Age Day 17 Moon Sign Taurus*

You have what it takes to attract just the right sort of company today, which means getting on in life, something that is of great importance to you while the Sun occupies its present position in your chart. If you don't manage to find very much time for pleasantries today, you can at least show kindness and compassion.

22 TUESDAY ☿ *Moon Age Day 18 Moon Sign Gemini*

What really sets you apart right now is your ability to speak out in front of others, and to elicit the necessary responses. This is nothing particularly new, but is a quality much enhanced by present planetary trends. In a business sense, you need to be ready to capitalise on new ideas at all stages today.

23 WEDNESDAY ☿ *Moon Age Day 19 Moon Sign Gemini*

You are ready for almost any challenge life can throw at you, plus a few you invent for yourself. All the same, you don't have to go tilting at windmills, just in order to get some excitement into your life. If you haven't enough to do, why not see whether there are people close by who would welcome a helping hand?

24 THURSDAY ☿ *Moon Age Day 20 Moon Sign Gemini*

In money matters, your present ability to think quickly should prove extremely useful. Even if you are not gambling in the generally accepted sense of the word, you might be willing to take a chance that could lead to greater monetary strength further down the line. Make time to enjoy yourself later in the day.

25 FRIDAY ☿ *Moon Age Day 21 Moon Sign Cancer*

The Sun has moved on and now inhabits the second house of your solar chart. For the next three or four weeks you are encouraged to place a stronger emphasis on material possessions than has been the case for the last month. Getting things looking the way you want at home would also suit the present interlude.

26 SATURDAY ☿ *Moon Age Day 22 Moon Sign Cancer*

There may not be time to do everything you have planned today, but you should at least be determined to try. Confidence remains highlighted, particularly when you are dealing with subject matter that is familiar to you. Your creative potential is especially strong, and you can demonstrate this through all facets of life.

27 SUNDAY ☿ *Moon Age Day 23 Moon Sign Leo*

The challenge today is to keep one step ahead of the competition. This is as true at work as it is in more social or sporting situations. Don't be surprised if not everyone proves to be adept at expressing either their opinions or their wishes today. A good deal of second-guessing may be necessary in order to address the situation.

28 MONDAY ☿ *Moon Age Day 24 Moon Sign Leo*

There are new highlights on offer in love and romance. This might come as something of a shock to some Librans, particularly those who have placed such considerations firmly on the back burner during the last couple of weeks. The best way to avoid lethargy today is to pitch in and boost your own sense of achievement.

29 TUESDAY ☿ *Moon Age Day 25 Moon Sign Leo*

You could find a degree of restlessness pervading your life as October draws towards its close. Your best response is to find something different to do and maybe some alternative people to share events and activities with you. This part of the week can be interesting, though once again it depends on how much effort you put in.

30 WEDNESDAY ☿ *Moon Age Day 26 Moon Sign Virgo*

The planetary focus today is on your presently strong personality and the way others view it. Even those you mix with frequently may not be used to seeing the very determined Libra, so it's worth giving them a sign to let them know you haven't really changed at all. Nevertheless, remain specific in your intentions.

31 THURSDAY ☿ *Moon Age Day 27 Moon Sign Virgo*

Acquiring what you need from life generally represents one of your greatest strengths at present. This can be a very practical period and one during which the focus is on your energy and your irrepressible desire to succeed. If you can't take everyone down the road you want to follow, why not go it alone?

November

2013

1 FRIDAY ☿ *Moon Age Day 28 Moon Sign Libra*

Stand by to take advantage of a potentially lucky period. With the lunar high comes a sudden surge in the power of Mercury in your life. This assists you to talk with confidence, walk with certainty and attract a number of admirers. By all means give yourself a pat on the back for something you've done well – then move on!

2 SATURDAY ☿ *Moon Age Day 0 Moon Sign Libra*

The lunar high encourages you to redress a few balances and promotes a more centred attitude. Contacts with others should be less strained, and you can utilise the strong diplomatic skills that are the province of your zodiac sign. When it comes to money, you can afford to chance your arm at the moment.

3 SUNDAY ☿ *Moon Age Day 1 Moon Sign Scorpio*

Current planetary trends assist you to show your best qualities and help you to create a supportive, stable atmosphere, which is ideal for a Sunday. You have scope to find comfort at home, and might decide to put to one side that need for movement that has been so much a part of your nature across the last few weeks.

4 MONDAY ☿ *Moon Age Day 2 Moon Sign Scorpio*

There is no reason to hang back when it comes to good ideas. Simply put your mind to the task of inventing new possibilities. You are still in the mood to get ahead, and it's simply a question of finding people around who can be persuaded to lend a hand. Romance is available for young or young-at-heart Librans.

5 TUESDAY ☿ *Moon Age Day 3 Moon Sign Sagittarius*

There is nothing to be gained by making life difficult for others, especially that of your partner. Spending time on your own can work wonders, particularly if you're not in the best frame of mind. Creative potential continues to be well accented, and you can use this to cheer up your home or even to tackle a new hobby.

6 WEDNESDAY ☿ *Moon Age Day 4 Moon Sign Sagittarius*

This would be an ideal time to seek new answers to old problems, since your ability to think things through is to the fore. You are also in a position to increase your level of popularity. Prepare to identify those around you who share your enthusiasm for life, and convince them to join in and have fun with you.

7 THURSDAY ☿ *Moon Age Day 5 Moon Sign Capricorn*

The Sun, presently in your solar second house, is a favourable influence for building on fresh starts that are already under way, or plans you choose to put into action now. At work you need to consider the impression you are making on superiors. Remember, there other people who genuinely want you to get on.

8 FRIDAY ☿ *Moon Age Day 6 Moon Sign Capricorn*

Your best approach to professional obligations today is to proceed in a quiet and organised way. Social matters are a different matter! Once the necessary routines are out of the way, you have a chance to let your hair down and have a good time. In a financial sense it's a question of discovering ways to gain more control.

9 SATURDAY ☿ *Moon Age Day 7 Moon Sign Aquarius*

Do you feel there hasn't been time of late to do everything you had wished? Even if today is busy too, you ought to be able to spare some moments to do someone a good turn. Offering help and advice is part of the Libra nature, and today is no exception. The company of younger people might hold a particular appeal.

10 SUNDAY ☿ *Moon Age Day 8 Moon Sign Aquarius*

A potentially quieter day allows you to mull over events from the past. This tinge of nostalgia is fine, as long as you don't become too tied up with retrospective thinking. Social highlights are available later, and there is much to be said for taking the opportunity to focus on your commitment to family members.

11 MONDAY ☿ *Moon Age Day 9 Moon Sign Aquarius*

Any minor hitches early in the day could simply prove to you that the strictly practical is not your most favoured area this week. Life now is about going along with others and mixing different potentials to ensure that everyone has a good time. This would be an ideal day for shopping, and for showing that you have an eye for a bargain!

12 TUESDAY *Moon Age Day 10 Moon Sign Pisces*

The go-getting side of your nature should be more apparent today. Despite this, your sensitivity is also enhanced, especially in terms of the needs of both older and younger people. Showing that you are a good listener is part of what the day is about. As well as assisting others, you can gain much along the way.

13 WEDNESDAY *Moon Age Day 11 Moon Sign Pisces*

If you insist on keeping the pace of everyday life as brisk as ever, finding time to simply be yourself could be quite difficult. Don't get hung up about Christmas just yet, even if the world is telling you that it is just around the corner. The more variety you can bring into your life today, the better you should feel.

14 THURSDAY *Moon Age Day 12 Moon Sign Aries*

For the next day or two you would be wise to put specific aspects of life on hold. Although there's nothing wrong with thinking big, the chance of actually moving forward is not helped by the presence of the lunar low. This is one occasion on which putting things off for a few days can work wonders.

15 FRIDAY *Moon Age Day 13 Moon Sign Aries*

A new period of domestic rewards is on offer. Venus gives you every assistance to get on especially well with family members and to gain from their company. This would be an ideal opportunity to address any recent tensions at home and to find ways to put them right once and for all.

16 SATURDAY *Moon Age Day 14 Moon Sign Taurus*

Social discussions and meetings can now bring enlightenment, and it's worth seeking the company of interesting types. New friendships become possible at this time, and there may also be a renewed fresh approach to existing ties. Almost anyone could have the ability to move you because you are presently so sensitive.

17 SUNDAY *Moon Age Day 15 Moon Sign Taurus*

The further you are able to go today, the better you should feel. This is true in terms of actual journeys you might choose to take, but also with regard to specific issues that you decide to push beyond previous limits. You needn't allow anyone or anything to hold you back during this most important interlude.

18 MONDAY *Moon Age Day 16 Moon Sign Taurus*

Professional matters can be a real labour of love today, which can be some consolation if they are not offering too much in the way of financial remuneration. Be patient, as you will have a chance to improve monetary matters in due course – but not just yet. All the same, be sure to check your lottery ticket carefully!

19 TUESDAY *Moon Age Day 17 Moon Sign Gemini*

There is a warning around today not to listen to the tall tales of others, and at the same time be careful you are not spreading any gossip yourself. If you need to know something, it would be far better to check out the details directly. You can be quite creative now, and should be willing to use this in all your daily tasks.

20 WEDNESDAY *Moon Age Day 18 Moon Sign Gemini*

As far as personal and emotional security are concerned, today is about ensuring you are well looked after. In terms of your nature, you have what it takes to be charming and well co-ordinated at the moment – with just the right attitude that is necessary to get on well in life. Don't forget to show your wisdom too.

21 THURSDAY *Moon Age Day 19 Moon Sign Cancer*

In practical matters, you need to keep your eye on the ball. This is not a time to diversify too much, and concentration is all-important. If you feel that family members are not taking their own responsibilities quite as seriously as they should, this might be the right time to let them know – gently!

22 FRIDAY *Moon Age Day 20 Moon Sign Cancer*

You can use your home situation to help you redress the balance at work, particularly if you are extremely active. Use some of your spare hours to quite simply have a rest and don't take on any more tasks than are strictly necessary at this time. Avoid getting on the wrong side of anyone who is in a position of influence.

23 SATURDAY *Moon Age Day 21 Moon Sign Leo*

A combination of leisure and romance ought to appeal today, in those moments when you are not busy working. If you want to avoid becoming bored, it would be sensible to deliberately make alterations to your routines. There is no point in worrying too much at the moment, unless it's about a lack of excitement.

24 SUNDAY *Moon Age Day 22 Moon Sign Leo*

With the Sun having moved from the second to the third house of your chart, this is the best time of all to allow yourself to be utterly ambitious in your attitude. A favourable weekend to focus clearly on a range of issues, including the direction your life is taking. For the moment it pays to think, but not act.

25 MONDAY *Moon Age Day 23 Moon Sign Leo*

Now you should be able to get your ideas across to others and to make a positive impression on the world at large. It could feel as though you have suddenly heard the starter's gun, as you race ahead, particularly in practical matters. Romantically speaking, letting someone know how you feel is the name of the game.

26 TUESDAY *Moon Age Day 24 Moon Sign Virgo*

It is possible that you are less socially inclined today, probably because the Moon is in your solar twelfth house. This encourages an interlude that is far quieter than of late – and more contemplative too. Be sure to let close friends, as well as your partner, know that you are not sulking about anything.

27 WEDNESDAY *Moon Age Day 25 Moon Sign Virgo*

This is a better time than most if you have decided to retreat from events a little and think things through more deeply. Of course the world makes certain demands of you that you cannot avoid, but meditation should still be possible. Ask others to take some of the strain and recharge flagging batteries.

28 THURSDAY *Moon Age Day 26 Moon Sign Libra*

Now your foot should be on the gas pedal of life as you begin to move forward in a very progressive way. The lunar high offers better general luck and ways to utilise all those good ideas that are floating around in your mind. Taking the odd chance can be fun, though financial speculation isn't to be recommended.

29 FRIDAY *Moon Age Day 27 Moon Sign Libra*

You have a chance to make yourself the centre of attention today, which is why it would be sensible to line up in your mind all those things you would wish others to do for you. It isn't being selfish to make use of your popularity, and in any case most of the people you approach for help should be more than happy to oblige.

Very thin, waning moon to E of South at 7.15am.

30 SATURDAY *Moon Age Day 28 Moon Sign Libra*

Make sure colleagues and friends notice how talkative, inquisitive and extremely friendly you are at the moment. The level of good luck available is still high, assisting you to go a step further than would normally be the case. Love and romance wait around the corner for Librans who are actively seeking either.

Moon was well visible at 7.15am at dawn. I last saw it through binoculars over North Hill summit at around 10.15am whilst sitting on my 59 BW bed. IT WAS NOT VISIBLE TO NAKED EYE. Despite driving round West Malvern I could not find it again although it should have been visible for some time.

December

2013

Anticyclonic gloom am.

1 SUNDAY *Moon Age Day 29 Moon Sign Scorpio*

You can definitely benefit from getting out and about. Being held in the same place all the time will probably hold little appeal at present, and you can afford to be quite definite in your attitude regarding personal freedom. If you make sure the people you meet today understand your point of view, they are more likely to offer support.

2 MONDAY *Moon Age Day 0 Moon Sign Scorpio*

There are signs that Libra could be taking an 'easy come, easy go' attitude towards money at present. This is probably just as well because, with Christmas close at hand, there's a risk of spending more than you intended. Be prepared to take some time out to really understand what makes your partner tick.

3 TUESDAY *Moon Age Day 1 Moon Sign Sagittarius*

New moon 00.22

Teamwork matters count for a great deal at present, which is why you should be willing to co-operate, even with people you haven't seen eye to eye with in the past. You can't expect to get everything you want from life at present, especially in a financial sense, though you might get close in at least some cases.

4 WEDNESDAY *Moon Age Day 2 Moon Sign Sagittarius*

When it comes to wit and intelligence, it appears that few can better you at present, and this can definitely help to boost your popularity. Such a trend has to be good with Christmas just around the corner, and it might also assist some Libran subjects in their efforts to advance at work.

5 THURSDAY *Moon Age Day 3 Moon Sign Capricorn*

A potentially hectic period in your personal life begins around this time. Of course, Christmas is fast approaching, and you might be starting to get in the mood, even though it's only the start of the month. Socially speaking, fighting shy of people you don't know very well would be understandable just now.

6 FRIDAY *Moon Age Day 4 Moon Sign Capricorn*

Keep your eyes and ears open for significant new input today and don't turn down the chance to do something different. The spotlight is on your curiosity, your instinctive need to know what makes things tick, so getting to the very heart of any matter is likely to be a priority. A day to show others how fascinating you can be.

7 SATURDAY *Moon Age Day 5 Moon Sign Aquarius*

Personal and intimate matters give you the chance to show your best side at this time. Concentrating on the family, rather than distant friends or even work, would certainly be no bad thing. If you find yourself facing a mountain of work, the best approach is to break it down into easily manageable units.

8 SUNDAY *Moon Age Day 6 Moon Sign Aquarius*

Even on a Sunday, professional demands could be quite irritating, especially if you have to deal with people who appear to be hopeless. Your usual Libran patience should be present, though perhaps not in great measure. What will work is your sense of humour. It's time to find laughter in every situation.

9 MONDAY *Moon Age Day 7 Moon Sign Pisces*

What you may find out in group situations today could prove to be extremely useful in the end. Listen to what is being said and don't commit yourself to joining in unless you are very sure of your ground. If you feel particularly fatigued at this time, there is nothing at all wrong with taking a short break.

10 TUESDAY *Moon Age Day 8 Moon Sign Pisces*

You can now benefit from the diversity of interests that are so typical of the Air-sign Libran nature. With more energy at your disposal and the chance to put it to good use, this is an ideal time to tackle all manner of new jobs. Your willingness to offer help and advice to others is noteworthy at the moment.

11 WEDNESDAY *Moon Age Day 9 Moon Sign Aries*

Confidence could sag somewhat as the lunar low arrives, but you don't have to give in to this tendency. Decide from the start that you are going to enjoy this quieter period and to use it to the best of your ability. Quiet pursuits are the order of the day, and can bring a degree of relaxation and even joy.

12 THURSDAY *Moon Age Day 10 Moon Sign Aries*

You need to be prepared to contend with certain limitations at the present time. This may not go down well, particularly if you are feeling a great deal of urgency within your nature at this time. Try to go with the flow in social matters, and listen specifically to what others are saying in family situations.

13 FRIDAY *Moon Age Day 11 Moon Sign Taurus*

This has potential to be a more than agreeable period. Venus is strong in your solar chart, assisting you to promote good relations in and around your home and domestic life. This is a very positive influence to have approaching Christmas time, and can be especially useful if you wish to create a traditional festive celebration.

14 SATURDAY *Moon Age Day 12 Moon Sign Taurus*

There is a very strong concern today with getting things done. Maybe you are too caught up with the details and fail to notice the importance of the sheer effort you are putting in? You need time to contemplate your actions and to come to terms with the slightly altered perceptions of loved ones.

15 SUNDAY *Moon Age Day 13 Moon Sign Taurus*

Emotional rewards are now there for the taking. In discussions related to work you will need to have the courage of your convictions, though this is not necessarily the case at home. It's important to finish off any outstanding tasks and, if possible, make the most of social possibilities that are on offer this evening.

16 MONDAY *Moon Age Day 14 Moon Sign Gemini*

Beware of overestimating your capacity for work. Although you have plenty of energy available in general this month, there are signs that today could be an exception. Why not pace yourself and allow others to take some of the strain? Remember that you need time to recover – ready for tomorrow's exertions!

17 TUESDAY *Moon Age Day 15 Moon Sign Gemini*

If you are faced with any slightly risky situations, you can afford to back your intuition at the moment. It isn't like Libra to take great chances, but you may decide that calculated ones are acceptable. There is also a focus today on money matters, and on how you deal with the necessities of Christmas.

18 WEDNESDAY *Moon Age Day 16 Moon Sign Cancer*

Trends encourage fruitful encounters with a number of different individuals today, some of whom may be able to offer the sort of information that is both timely and useful. Where love and romance are concerned, it shouldn't be difficult to find the right words to sweep someone off their feet under present planetary influences.

19 THURSDAY *Moon Age Day 17 Moon Sign Cancer*

A sense of urgency is all very well, but it could be misplaced today. It's important to recognise the progress you are making in various aspects of life, even if some of them are not coming good quite as quickly as you wish. Stay aware of the needs of family members, especially those of your partner.

20 FRIDAY *Moon Age Day 18 Moon Sign Cancer*

You have a chance to gain great fulfilment today through your family. Getting on positively in terms of your career is a different matter, though you should be able to address any problems in this area. Socially speaking, it's time for Libra to get the festive season well under way!

21 SATURDAY *Moon Age Day 19 Moon Sign Leo*

Your fun-loving nature is stimulated by present planetary trends, giving you the opportunity to show the joker inside you at almost every turn. There's no reason to hold back in any situation, simply because you doubt the reaction of colleagues. If you have things to say, you can persuade the world to lend an ear.

22 SUNDAY *Moon Age Day 20 Moon Sign Leo*

You can take advantage of an influx of bright new ideas, and need to ensure you have a positive audience. Your usual ways of relaxing might not fit the bill at present, and it is entirely possible that you will be looking for new ways to pep up your social hours, particularly this evening.

23 MONDAY *Moon Age Day 21 Moon Sign Virgo*

Emotive issues in relationships take centre stage for some Libran subjects today. Don't be too ready to allow these a great deal of room in your mind. It is possible that you are not being anywhere near as rational as you could be. Once again, you need to take a longer-term view of situations.

24 TUESDAY *Moon Age Day 22 Moon Sign Virgo*

This certainly has potential to be a very positive time when it comes to pleasing family members and friends alike. All the same, you can consider this to be your special day during the Christmas break, and it's worth finding ways to do the things that really appeal to you. This might include spending at least some time alone.

25 WEDNESDAY *Moon Age Day 23 Moon Sign Virgo*

Be willing to open your eyes to something wonderful today, despite the necessary tasks of a Christmas Day. If you're spending time with family members, turning your mind to future holidays would be no bad thing. Whatever you are thinking today, there is a long-term aspect about it that brightens the day no end.

26 THURSDAY *Moon Age Day 24 Moon Sign Libra*

If ever there was a time when it was possible for you to talk anyone into anything, that day has come. The lunar high, together with Mercury's position in your solar chart, enhances your silver tongue and your tremendous influence. Now is the time to feather your own nest materially, and to help others on the way.

27 FRIDAY *Moon Age Day 25 Moon Sign Libra*

Another family high spot when you can allow your sense of absolute joy to shine out like the sun. You can capitalise on your popularity at this time, which is always stimulating to the Libran personality. In the full swing of the party season, this is no time to be running out of steam or seeking places to be quiet.

28 SATURDAY *Moon Age Day 26 Moon Sign Scorpio*

Group-based activities may hold some potential rewards. There are some frustrations to be dealt with now, particularly if you are unable to get the world going in the way you would wish until after the beginning of the New Year. The Christmas break can seem too long for all the Air signs, of which you are one.

29 SUNDAY *Moon Age Day 27 Moon Sign Scorpio*

Relationships could well have their ups and downs at the moment, and it's worth asking yourself whether you have been spending too much time in the company of one specific individual. The spotlight is also on your level of consumption. Abstinence is not necessary, though a little circumspection might help.

30 MONDAY *Moon Age Day 28 Moon Sign Sagittarius*

It's important to mix with as many different sorts of people today as proves to be possible. You have a chance to come up with a number of quite innovative ideas. The next step is to find individuals who will listen to what you have to say and who can even be persuaded to help you to push forward progressively.

31 TUESDAY *Moon Age Day 29 Moon Sign Sagittarius*

The last day of the year offers an opportunity to create fun and diversity. The emphasis is now firmly on humour, conversation and good company, and it's up to you to seek out all of these. Beware of taking anything too seriously at present, and be willing to enjoy whatever party is taking place.

LIBRA:
2014 DIARY PAGES

LIBRA: YOUR YEAR IN BRIEF

This has potential to be an interesting start to the year as far as you are concerned. You are more definite than usual and you might even be able to surprise quite a few people. Both January and February offer new and fascinating diversions and both months should also be better than average when it comes to romance. Exercise a little caution regarding money and save what you can because you may have more opportunities to travel during the coming year than are sometimes available.

March and April promise much but don't always quite deliver in the way you would wish. More effort is needed if you want to achieve all your objectives, but you can help yourself a great deal if you allow others to intervene on your behalf. Routines are definitely for the birds, especially during April, and the more you are willing to be spontaneous, the better the period is likely to be. On a positive note, things might be stronger in terms of your personal finances.

It looks as though May and June will offer you yet more in the way of material gains, and could also be a chance for you to get closer to achieving some longed-for objectives. You will still be acting on impulse for much of the time and although you might occasionally have cause to regret the fact, in the main this way of being works well. It's time to spoil yourself in some way, and if that means spending a few pounds on something you know to be an indulgence, so be it.

July and August see the world warming up, and you have scope to bring a great deal of heat into your life too. This is the time when you sizzle romantically. Librans who have been looking for love need to concentrate their efforts during the summer holiday season and it is also possible that you will have unexpected opportunities for travel. People from the past make a new entry into your life and could bring with them a few surprises. Don't be too quick to judge the actions of a friend in August.

September and October are invariably good months for you because this is the period during which the Sun returns to your part of the zodiac. Objectives are easier to fulfil and people come good with their promises. You won't be held back where your plans are concerned, and should be much more definite than usual in your opinions. Not everyone will think you are the tops during this progressive phase, but the people that count should be on your side.

Be bold, brave and even bumptious towards the end of the year. Allow your personality to shine through November and December and light up the world like a Christmas tree. You have so much to offer but you too often allow circumstances and people to get in your way. This is a period to show everyone what you are capable of, and you won't hesitate. Christmas should be a period of extreme fun – but also possible exhaustion!

January

2014

1 WEDNESDAY *Moon Age Day 0 Moon Sign Capricorn*

Personal triumphs you can achieve around now enable you to take a great leap forward, at least in terms of your own ego. Even if you don't stand to make a lot of money or gain significant influence, what really matters is that you believe in yourself more. The attitude of friends could be very surprising.

2 THURSDAY *Moon Age Day 1 Moon Sign Capricorn*

Personal influence is highlighted now, and it's clear that you have what it takes to make the best possible impression when it counts the most. Confidence might lag behind early in the day, but it shouldn't be long before you can ensure you are flavour of the month, at least for a certain group of people. A favourable day for romance.

3 FRIDAY *Moon Age Day 2 Moon Sign Aquarius*

A work situation can assist you to put yourself in the picture and could lead to further advances of a sort you hadn't been expecting. There are many potential surprises around at the moment and these can justify the confidence you have had for a while now. Creative potential is also well accented under present planetary influences.

4 SATURDAY *Moon Age Day 3 Moon Sign Aquarius*

Be ready to respond to suggestions from others that you change your outlook. There's nothing wrong with accommodating them if you can, though a more fixed attitude than would normally be the case is indicated for Libra at present. You could try to at least give the impression that you are taking other people's opinions into account.

5 SUNDAY *Moon Age Day 4 Moon Sign Pisces*

High spots are once again available where romance is concerned and you will want to make the very best of what the planets have to offer in this regard. Even if you are not involved in a romantic attachment at the moment, it might be only a matter of time before you're able to take advantage of some favourable opportunities in this direction.

6 MONDAY *Moon Age Day 5 Moon Sign Pisces*

Keep your eyes and ears open to discover what is going on in your immediate vicinity. Even listening to gossip can be rewarding at the moment and might lead you towards actions that will help you to become better off in some way. Be prepared to welcome personalities into your life now, and to make the most of the interesting interludes they offer.

7 TUESDAY *Moon Age Day 6 Moon Sign Aries*

Today marks the arrival of the lunar low, which is that part of each month when the Moon occupies your opposite zodiac sign. This does little for your self-belief, and might make you prone to the odd mistake. By all means be bold and determined when it is possible, but also recognise the fact that there are limitations around just now.

8 WEDNESDAY *Moon Age Day 7 Moon Sign Aries*

Hearth and home could now offer you the best possibilities, as is the case for some days to come. Even if you are still doing what is necessary out there in the wider world, there is much to be said for basing your sense of security on what you know the best. It's worth being mindful of the opinions of your friends at this time.

9 THURSDAY *Moon Age Day 8 Moon Sign Aries*

You are still encouraged to seek warmth and security in your home life, so much so that this may seem preferable to putting in that extra bit of effort out there in the big, wide world. There's no need to accept second-best, either from yourself or from people who are not doing as well as they might. Routines could be something of a chore.

10 FRIDAY *Moon Age Day 9 Moon Sign Taurus*

The more expressive aspects of your nature are very much to the fore today, and you shouldn't have any trouble getting your message across to anyone. This helps you to increase your popularity and ensures that the world at large notices that you are around. Don't worry about the odd mistake today because you have everything you need to overcome them.

11 SATURDAY *Moon Age Day 10 Moon Sign Taurus*

The focus is now once again on home and family, but this is a more temporary situation than was the case a few days ago. For today at least there are good reasons to withdraw into yourself somewhat, and you need to decide whether you have any real desire to pit your wits against others.

12 SUNDAY *Moon Age Day 11 Moon Sign Gemini*

Success today is about making a suitably strong impact when it matters the most, in preparation for a very positive start to a new working week. Rather than hiding your abilities at this time, it's a question of showing that you can come up with the goods when necessary. Bear in mind that this is a chance to impress potentially influential people.

13 MONDAY *Moon Age Day 12 Moon Sign Gemini*

Do you feel that those close to you understand what you really need from life? If they do, you ought to be able to gain some valuable support from them when it truly matters. Be brave about approaching situations that might have made you shake in your boots earlier. It's time to show that you can tackle almost anything.

14 TUESDAY *Moon Age Day 13 Moon Sign Gemini*

It might appear now that others are getting ahead much faster than you are. This is a very temporary state of affairs and is not something you should allow to trouble you too much. One option is to ask others to take some of the strain, and you needn't be shy about asking for help, especially from people who are in your debt in any case.

15 WEDNESDAY *Moon Age Day 14 Moon Sign Cancer*

Your mental focus may not be at its best today, and as a result this might not be an ideal time for major decision-making. Why not allow others to make some of the running while you take a back seat? In many ways this gives you a chance to clear the decks for the sort of action that will be possible soon.

16 THURSDAY *Moon Age Day 15 Moon Sign Cancer*

Most social relationships remain well marked, but that doesn't mean there won't be the odd person around today who gives you something of a problem. You get on best with those who cope well with your vibrant and changeable nature, and it might be difficult to deal with situations in which someone is trying to pull you up in your tracks.

17 FRIDAY *Moon Age Day 16 Moon Sign Leo*

You can't expect everything you have to say to go down well with everyone you meet today. Being keen to get your ideas across is all very well, though it's important to avoid being brusque at the moment in the way you say things. A large dollop of diplomacy might go a long way, and this comes easily to you.

18 SATURDAY *Moon Age Day 17 Moon Sign Leo*

Even if you ensure that your attitude is just as friendly and every bit as communicative as usual, it may still be difficult to score universal successes, particularly if there are awkward people around who you have to deal with very carefully. Make the most of any interactions with people from the past, and of the opportunities such relationships offer.

19 SUNDAY *Moon Age Day 18 Moon Sign Leo*

This is a favourable period for your love life, and a Sunday that offers a chance to seek warmth and comfort with your partner or sweetheart. The time is right to put the very best side of Libra on display and to call in a few favours from people who would be only too willing to put themselves out on your behalf.

20 MONDAY *Moon Age Day 19 Moon Sign Virgo*

If people all around are making their own demands on you, it may be difficult to find too much time for personal contemplation. This has potential to be one of the busiest days of the month, and you need to be very organised if you are going to get through everything. The advice is to avoid family arguments like the plague.

21 TUESDAY *Moon Age Day 20 Moon Sign Virgo*

When it comes to getting your own way the planets are standing in the right position to assist you at the moment. This shouldn't mean that you have to bulldoze others with your ideas, but that you can use the sort of persistence that will wear them down. Advancement at work should be within your grasp more now than at any other time during January.

22 WEDNESDAY *Moon Age Day 21 Moon Sign Libra*

The bigger you think, the better you should be acting today. This is the time of the lunar high, the two- or three-day period each month during which the Moon occupies your own zodiac sign of Libra. It's a time to be right on the ball and ready to address almost any issue that comes into your mind. Be decisive whenever possible.

23 THURSDAY *Moon Age Day 22 Moon Sign Libra*

You might not take too kindly to people who cross you or who show a lack of confidence in your decisions. All the same, being too impetuous is not to be recommended at the moment, so it wouldn't do any harm to listen to what is being said. In any case, it's better to know what others think than have them talking behind your back.

24 FRIDAY *Moon Age Day 23 Moon Sign Scorpio*

It appears that you can now be at your best when dealing with groups rather than individuals. It's a question of showing other people how inspirational you can be, and persuading them to follow your lead in various circumstances. There are also gains to be made on a personal level and a better understanding to be reached with family members.

25 SATURDAY *Moon Age Day 24 Moon Sign Scorpio*

It is important today to read the small print, no matter what you are doing. An impulsive streak can sometimes get you into trouble, and that's something you need to avoid right now. The fact is that Libra is sometimes too trusting. Recognising that some individuals are working against your interests can really make the difference now.

26 SUNDAY *Moon Age Day 25 Moon Sign Scorpio*

It might be necessary to show your assertive side today, and that could come as something of a surprise to certain other people. It doesn't do any harm now and again for you to lay down the law. The problem is that you can sometimes be too easy-going for your own good. Making people laugh should be a natural aspect of life at the moment.

27 MONDAY *Moon Age Day 26 Moon Sign Sagittarius*

Actions definitely do speak louder than words at the beginning of this new working week. If you want something done, there is much to be said for at least starting it yourself. It's possible for you to influence those around you with your enthusiasm, and to encourage them by demonstrating that you are willing to get your own hands dirty.

28 TUESDAY *Moon Age Day 27 Moon Sign Sagittarius*

The spotlight is now on the especially innovative ideas you can come up with around this time, and it's worth discussing these with others as much as proves to be possible. Thinking up a novel way to do something is meat and drink to you, and you have what it takes to break tasks down into their component parts.

29 WEDNESDAY *Moon Age Day 28 Moon Sign Capricorn*

Arguments might not get you very far at the moment, whereas explaining your point of view fully is much more likely to succeed. This could well test your patience no end, particularly if there are people around who refuse to listen, no matter how diplomatic you try to be. It's time to keep your cool.

30 THURSDAY *Moon Age Day 29 Moon Sign Capricorn*

Capitalise on new potential that is within your grasp. There are gains to be made by finding plenty to keep you occupied, both at work and later when you choose to enjoy yourself. A word of warning: it might be advisable to think very carefully about every new strategy and decide whether you can actually deal with them all at the same time.

31 FRIDAY *Moon Age Day 0 Moon Sign Aquarius*

Even if life has its complications at the moment, you needn't allow these to hold you up for very long. Trends assist you to remain very organised inside your own head, although the only slight fly in the ointment might be organising the people with whom you are mixing. Make sure there is plenty of humour about today.

February

2014

1 SATURDAY *Moon Age Day 1 Moon Sign Aquarius*

Once again it's important to stay on the ball and to make sure you show the full extent of your abilities to anyone in a position of authority over you. You can afford to seek any support you need from friends, and you may find that one or two of them are anxious to repay a favour they had from you some time ago.

2 SUNDAY *Moon Age Day 2 Moon Sign Pisces*

There's nothing wrong with keeping busy, though that doesn't mean you have to ignore your social life, which also has its importance. Family members and friends alike could give you reason to be proud for much of the coming week, and you might also have an opportunity to play a small part in someone else's success.

3 MONDAY *Moon Age Day 3 Moon Sign Pisces*

If you really want to get on well today you should be prepared to ring the changes and to make each little job as rewarding and fresh as the last. The emphasis is on your ability to persuade others to fall in line with your alterations, and on your willingness to seek help when required. The natural charm of Libra can work wonders now.

4 TUESDAY *Moon Age Day 4 Moon Sign Aries*

You might just as well get used to the idea that a slower pace of life is required under the lunar low, because for all the effort you expound there may be little gained today. Why not plan ahead and use this time to clear the decks for action later? One option is to catch up on conversations with family members or good friends.

5 WEDNESDAY *Moon Age Day 5 Moon Sign Aries*

Uphill challenges are part of what today is about, and it's important to recognise that you might not have what it takes to sort everything out for yourself. It's worth seeking support from the people you trust the most, though there's nothing at all wrong with relying on strangers more than you would usually do.

6 THURSDAY *Moon Age Day 6 Moon Sign Taurus*

You need to appreciate just how much love surrounds you at this time. This can help you to feel warm inside and spur you on to even greater success on behalf of the people you care about the most. Stand by to make the most of a slightly quieter period at this stage of the working week, but don't be afraid to instigate some upheaval.

7 FRIDAY ☿ *Moon Age Day 7 Moon Sign Taurus*

Co-operation is the key to success, and this applies just as much to social and romantic possibilities as it does to your work. There's no doubt that trends assist you to become the leader of the pack at present, but what proves to be even more important is your ability to delegate – if only because you can't do everything yourself.

8 SATURDAY ☿ *Moon Age Day 8 Moon Sign Gemini*

The more you seek out the company of people you genuinely like, the greater are the potential successes of today. Some of these could be social in nature, particularly if you are willing to put down the reins of professional progress for the weekend. Don't be surprised if you find family members both intriguing and slightly frustrating!

9 SUNDAY ☿ *Moon Age Day 9 Moon Sign Gemini*

What sets today apart is not any gains you make if you are working, but rather what you achieve once the responsibilities of the day are out of the way. For real success you need to mix business with pleasure. On the way you have scope to gain allies who will be of tremendous use to you in the weeks and months to come.

10 MONDAY ☿ *Moon Age Day 10 Moon Sign Gemini*

You needn't allow much to stand in your way right now, though be ready to deal with the odd person who doesn't respond in a positive way to what you are doing. Your best approach during the current interlude is to stick to your guns and make it plain that you are not a person to be crossed. Even Libra has a temper.

11 TUESDAY ☿ *Moon Age Day 11 Moon Sign Cancer*

Great things can happen today if you are willing to express your innermost feelings and if you respond positively to the things others have to say. Romance is especially well starred, and Libran people who have been looking for a new love could do worse than to concentrate their efforts around this time.

12 WEDNESDAY ☿ *Moon Age Day 12 Moon Sign Cancer*

Hard work pays dividends and you can make significant progress, particularly if you are able to make full use of your natural ingenuity. Acting on impulse is the name of the game at present, and your spontaneous attitude is potentially infectious. Ignore any negative influences brought about by people who are pessimistic.

13 THURSDAY ☿ *Moon Age Day 13 Moon Sign Leo*

Even if this is a slightly quieter day, it still offers good opportunities for some advancement. It's all about looking at situations carefully and taking quite a contemplative approach. Today is more suited to planning than action, but in the longer term this could well turn out to have been a very good thing.

14 FRIDAY ☿ *Moon Age Day 14 Moon Sign Leo*

Confidence remains generally well marked, even if you don't always feel yourself capable of achieving what others expect. Stretching yourself is important because it offers you a chance to learn things about your own nature that you might not have suspected. Be prepared to change social arrangements at short notice whenever you feel it is necessary.

15 SATURDAY ☿ *Moon Age Day 15 Moon Sign Leo*

If you are not entirely sure what direction your personal life is taking, the best way forward is to simply wait and see. Trends suggest that not everyone may be behaving quite as you expect, and as a result you may need to be flexible. Responding to situations at short notice can sometimes be difficult for Libra, but it's par for the course right now.

16 SUNDAY ☿ *Moon Age Day 16 Moon Sign Virgo*

It shouldn't be hard to find good company today, particularly if you make it clear you are looking for it. Make the most of every positive trend that surrounds you and don't hold back when it comes to expressing your opinions. It's time for you to show how bright, energetic and magnetic you can be, and to capitalise on this significant period.

17 MONDAY ☿ *Moon Age Day 17 Moon Sign Virgo*

You have scope to make events at work slightly more profitable than you had been expecting. This means applying yourself to whatever task seems to be most important, though you can afford to find time later for having fun. If the attitude of your partner takes some working out later in the day, simply turn on your usual Libran patience.

18 TUESDAY ☿ *Moon Age Day 18 Moon Sign Libra*

With the arrival of the lunar high today there is very little that cannot be achieved if you simply adopt the right attitude. Good luck is available, and you have scope to turn this into one of the most financially fortunate days of the month. There's an emphasis on getting things done immediately, so it may be difficult to have patience with those who dilly-dally.

19 WEDNESDAY ☿ *Moon Age Day 19 Moon Sign Libra*

The positive trends continue, and there isn't much point in waiting around for the rest of the world to catch up in a practical sense. It's time to decide what you want from life and work out how you are going to get it. Social trends are the best of all, making this a favourable interlude for finding ways to bring people out of their shells.

20 THURSDAY ☿ *Moon Age Day 20 Moon Sign Libra*

Domestic matters have the potential to keep you smiling, and with plenty to play for, the horizon looks positive. Today works best if you remain chatty and approachable, which isn't usually difficult for your zodiac sign, and you needn't allow any little problems to act as an irritant. This might be a good day for a short journey.

21 FRIDAY ☿ *Moon Age Day 21 Moon Sign Scorpio*

There is much to aim for at work, and ahead of the weekend it's also worth planning how you intend to enjoy yourself. Be willing to pace yourself as much as possible and don't take on too many jobs at the same time. Although little mistakes are possible today, you needn't allow any of them to derail your progress.

22 SATURDAY ☿ *Moon Age Day 22 Moon Sign Scorpio*

The focus right now should be moving to romantic attachments, even if you are also finding plenty to keep you busy in a practical sense. This is the perfect time to prove to the person you love the most just how important they are to your life, and trends give you all the assistance you need in order to do so today.

23 SUNDAY ☿ *Moon Age Day 23 Moon Sign Sagittarius*

An increase in your general level of luck can be detected around this time. This might be especially true in the financial area of life, though this is not a good time for gambling or taking too many chances. You will instinctively know whether you can afford to chance your arm – it's all a matter of intuition.

24 MONDAY ☿ *Moon Age Day 24 Moon Sign Sagittarius*

Keeping yourself very much on the go in a general sense is the order of the day, and you may not have much time to please yourself at the moment. Never mind, getting a great deal done can be useful, and can bring a sense of satisfaction before the day is out. Why not seek support from friends if you need it?

25 TUESDAY ☿ *Moon Age Day 25 Moon Sign Capricorn*

A family matter can act as a reminder of where your roots actually lie. Be prepared to offer support to relatives, and especially to younger family members if you can. You would be wise to avoid getting involved in any discussions that can have no logical conclusion, because it would probably just be a waste of time.

26 WEDNESDAY ☿ *Moon Age Day 26 Moon Sign Capricorn*

You certainly have what it takes to get yourself noticed at the moment, and shouldn't be taking a back seat in anything. The more arduous and demanding the task, the greater should be your desire to succeed. Sporting activities are well accented at this time, though as in other areas of life, you are a better team player than you are an individual champion.

27 THURSDAY ☿ *Moon Age Day 27 Moon Sign Aquarius*

There are planetary aspects around now that encourage you to take any issues that have troubled you for some time and put them in the past for good. This is also an excellent interlude in which to bury the hatchet over disagreements that have lasted too long. Your ability to deal with warring factions of any kind is particularly well marked at present.

28 FRIDAY ☿ *Moon Age Day 28 Moon Sign Aquarius*

A lively accent is around as far as important meetings are concerned, and it pays to do your best today to impress as many people as possible. If you make sure you display your usual cheerful and winning ways it should be easy for you to come across positively. It isn't hard for people to love Librans – it comes naturally!

March

2014

1 SATURDAY *Moon Age Day 0 Moon Sign Pisces*

Not only should you be taking pleasure from activities of all kinds at the start of the weekend, you also ought to surround yourself with stimulating company whenever you can. Contentment is there for the taking, but that needn't stop you from continuing to apply gentle pressure, especially regarding a family matter.

2 SUNDAY *Moon Age Day 1 Moon Sign Pisces*

There is much to be said for letting others know the way you are feeling, though that can mean speaking out when it might be slightly difficult to do so. Balancing between diplomacy and honesty may not be too easy for you at the moment. In the end, it's probably best to stick with honesty.

3 MONDAY *Moon Age Day 2 Moon Sign Aries*

Any apparent decline in your fortunes shouldn't cause too much concern. Difficult situations are the legacy of the lunar low, and there's no need to react to them more than is strictly necessary. You can still make use of today by tackling specific tasks, because it's important to keep plugging away, whatever the planetary situation.

4 TUESDAY *Moon Age Day 3 Moon Sign Aries*

Seeking out the company of others can make all the difference at this time, and this is an ideal day to socialise, even if you are adopting a slightly slower pace of life than you might have wished. The distractions that are around at this time suggest that concentrating fully on the tasks that lie before you may be far from easy.

5 WEDNESDAY *Moon Age Day 4 Moon Sign Taurus*

Influences at work only highlight the necessity for thinking ahead and planning carefully. Even if routines are something of a chore at the moment, in the main you have the ability to tackle your objectives in a fairly ordered way. Confidence to speak out is to the fore, and should assist you to advance in some way.

6 THURSDAY *Moon Age Day 5 Moon Sign Taurus*

Your ego is emphasised, giving you everything you need to make a definite impression. You can't expect everyone to understand the more forceful side of your nature, even if you make it clear that you are willing to make decisions. Others are used to you hedging your bets, and a very certain Libran is something that is a little unusual.

7 FRIDAY *Moon Age Day 6 Moon Sign Taurus*

Today is all about showing your most attractive features, and the position of Venus, your ruling planet, only encourages others to see the very best in you. Don't be too quick to make decisions until tomorrow. A considered approach works best in most areas of your life and this is particularly true where romance is concerned.

8 SATURDAY *Moon Age Day 7 Moon Sign Gemini*

In terms of money you should now be entering a fairly stable period. There are gains to be made, even in some unexpected directions, and you might also be able to increase your general earning power. Be ready to capitalise on the special compliments you manage to attract this Saturday.

9 SUNDAY *Moon Age Day 8 Moon Sign Gemini*

Trends encourage you to put your mind in overdrive and keep it working much faster than would normally be the case. This might not make it particularly easy for slower types to keep up with you, so a little patience would be no bad thing. It's sometimes difficult to understand why colleagues or even friends are so slow in understanding things that are self-evident to you.

Mum is 94 today!

10 MONDAY *Moon Age Day 9 Moon Sign Cancer*

Today should be favourable for adventure and travel – in fact, this is a theme that runs through the whole week. Even if you don't find every job easy at the moment, when it matters the most you should be able to make progress. It pays to keep in touch with people who are at a distance and to do your best to impress at work.

11 TUESDAY *Moon Age Day 10 Moon Sign Cancer*

You can improve your general efficiency at this time and make material gains as a result. This would be an ideal day to make contact with those you don't see too often, and to capitalise on the interesting information you can glean from them. It may be that relatives are less easy to deal with at the moment than friends.

12 WEDNESDAY *Moon Age Day 11 Moon Sign Cancer*

It appears that your ego is in the ascendant and you need to be sure that you are making the right sort of impression on the world at large. In a professional sense this might be somewhat difficult, though you shouldn't have any problem at all getting onside with new friends or impressing the ones you already have.

13 THURSDAY *Moon Age Day 12 Moon Sign Leo*

You have what it takes to put yourself at the head of the queue now, no matter what area of life you are addressing. It's a natural gift, brought to you by present planetary positions in your solar chart. A slightly quieter approach is encouraged tomorrow, so it's important to make as much progress right now as proves to be possible.

14 FRIDAY *Moon Age Day 13 Moon Sign Leo*

It's worth examining your views regarding certain matters and asking yourself whether you are being truly realistic. You are able to see through the haze that everyday life places over some issues, and what you discover might surprise you. Enlist the support of relatives or friends if you find that you are out of your depth in any way.

15 SATURDAY *Moon Age Day 14 Moon Sign Virgo*

This is a time to show as many people as you can what you are made of. For those of you who work on a Saturday, present trends are favourable for getting ahead of the competition, though you can achieve your objectives without falling out with anyone. Libra can afford to be all sociability and good intentions now.

16 SUNDAY *Moon Age Day 15 Moon Sign Virgo*

A complete change of scenery appears to be both possible and necessary today. This might be the first time you have realised that the spring has actually arrived, and it's important to ensure that you experience it for yourself and enjoy it. When it comes to romance, make sure you are at your brightest and best.

17 MONDAY *Moon Age Day 16 Moon Sign Virgo*

Material issues can contain a few pitfalls today, which is why you need to be especially careful, particularly with money. Don't be afraid to stand up for any friends who feel they are under attack because your presence in the situation can make all the difference. If you do argue at all today, make sure it is for others and not yourself.

18 TUESDAY *Moon Age Day 17 Moon Sign Libra*

Creating bigger and better opportunities now comes naturally, and there should be nothing left of the shrinking violet you might have seemed to be a few days ago. Take all the power of the lunar high and use it positively to make an excellent period of advancement. Other planets also come to this positive party.

19 WEDNESDAY *Moon Age Day 18 Moon Sign Libra*

There should be little or nothing to stand in your way today, and the amount of progress you make in life is at least partly down to your own attitude. Neither should you be short of something to do, though this is a time during which you have scope to tackle a number of jobs at the same time. Success is now within your reach.

20 THURSDAY *Moon Age Day 19 Moon Sign Scorpio*

It might be best to keep your options open today and not to be too specific about anything. Even if you know there are people around who are genuinely on your side, it's possible that others simply pretend to be. Telling the difference shouldn't be too difficult, at a time during which your intuition is especially well honed.

21 FRIDAY *Moon Age Day 20 Moon Sign Scorpio*

This has potential to be a positive time for most Libran people, especially in your personal or love life. It's always possible that you have given others the wrong message on occasions previously, though you needn't allow this to happen now. You have a very discriminating eye at present, which makes this an ideal time to buy things.

22 SATURDAY *Moon Age Day 21 Moon Sign Sagittarius*

Long-distance travel and intellectual exchanges are favoured at this time. You have an opportunity to seek out fresh fields and pastures new, and that's exactly what your astrological chart encourages. Don't be sold short regarding anything that rightfully belongs to you, and be willing to stick up for yourself.

23 SUNDAY *Moon Age Day 22 Moon Sign Sagittarius*

You have what it takes to go from strength to strength in terms of professional matters at the moment, though there's nothing wrong with taking a holiday from such thoughts today. Make Sunday your own and find ways to enjoy yourself, perhaps in the company of people you really like and who fire your imagination.

24 MONDAY *Moon Age Day 23 Moon Sign Capricorn*

An ideal time for fresh starts as far as your social life is concerned, and of course that might mean getting to know new people. Fortunately that's not a problem for a Libran, and you probably relish moving in new circles. One of the best aspects of this situation is your ability to gain respect from newcomers for both you and your opinions.

25 TUESDAY *Moon Age Day 24 Moon Sign Capricorn*

Seek out news on the personal front that will put you into a very positive frame of mind. Concern for family members and even friends might be high, but you need to ask whether it's actually justified. Instead of finding reasons to worry, look for positive and inspirational situations, which could be all around you now.

26 WEDNESDAY *Moon Age Day 25 Moon Sign Aquarius*

Any disappointments at the start of the day can be blown away like dead leaves on the wind once the second half of Wednesday comes along. Make sure you are right back on form by the evening and ready to make the best impression possible, especially in all social matters. The sound advice you offer others can work wonders now.

27 THURSDAY *Moon Age Day 26 Moon Sign Aquarius*

Make the most of a potentially beneficial period in terms of social commitments and the possibility of advancement in your career. Accepting help from others is all very well, though sorting out the wheat from the chaff is a prerequisite of today. Don't get bogged down with details that don't really matter, and keep your mind on the task in hand.

28 FRIDAY *Moon Age Day 27 Moon Sign Aquarius*

Make the most of any opportunities today to look back at the recent past and come to terms with certain emotional issues. Do away with any regrets because they are really no use to you at the moment. Some of the gains that are waiting in the wings might be significantly greater than you have been expecting.

29 SATURDAY *Moon Age Day 28 Moon Sign Pisces*

It pays to avoid people who sound too good to be true right now, because it's an odds-on certainty that they are. Before you can get down to doing what you really want today, be prepared to get a certain amount of dross out of the way. An early start would help, and this enables you to get on to the interesting stuff as soon as possible.

30 SUNDAY *Moon Age Day 29 Moon Sign Pisces*

Trends suggest an element of conflict for Libra today, perhaps with your partner or a family member. Your best response is to withdraw from such situations if you can. Better by far to bite your tongue for the moment, especially since you might be wrong. Tomorrow is another day, and you won't be so adamant by then.

31 MONDAY *Moon Age Day 0 Moon Sign Aries*

The lunar low is a time to stick around familiar places and faces if you can because that is where you are likely to feel most at ease. For once, spreading yourself too thinly won't appeal, which is unusual for Libra but is happening now in response to the position of the Moon. Contact with those you don't see too often could be beneficial.

April

2014

1 TUESDAY *Moon Age Day 1 Moon Sign Aries*

Health matters come under the spotlight at present, and it's important that you don't put too much pressure on yourself, especially when it comes to unnecessary stress. Be willing to look others in the eye and challenge their views, even if they are your superior. They shouldn't respect you any less for speaking your mind.

2 WEDNESDAY *Moon Age Day 2 Moon Sign Taurus*

Everything that is really important and meaningful about today centres around personal relationships and the way you are viewing them. Make the most of opportunities to make your partner happy. If you don't have a partner at the moment, this would be a favourable interlude in which to look for one.

3 THURSDAY *Moon Age Day 3 Moon Sign Taurus*

A boost to all communication issues is now on offer, giving you every assistance to get your message across, even when it's a complicated one. You have scope to shine in debates, or in any situation in which you are put on the spot. The only slight problem could occur if you don't have as much regard for yourself as others do for you.

4 FRIDAY *Moon Age Day 4 Moon Sign Gemini*

You can afford to feel happy with the general pace of life and still have scope to gain a great deal from the attitude and actions of loved ones. Even if this isn't the best financial day of the month, you can at least hold on to what you have and lay down plans for monetary improvements that come later.

5 SATURDAY *Moon Age Day 5 Moon Sign Gemini*

This would be a very good time to focus your attention on creative pursuits. Your strength lies in your ability to get others on your side and in your willingness to take charge of certain situations. Trying to balance the needs of those with whom you are in contact might prove a little difficult, but you should be able to manage well enough.

6 SUNDAY *Moon Age Day 6 Moon Sign Cancer*

An element of restlessness is indicated now, and you might decide that routines simply don't appeal. Libra has a need to break out and to look at life in quite a different way from others. Meeting new and inspiring people would be no bad thing, and it's important to show your sensitivity to the needs of family members, especially those who are younger than you.

7 MONDAY *Moon Age Day 7 Moon Sign Cancer*

You are now encouraged to put a significant amount of energy into personal relationships, both today and for the rest of this week. If this means that something more practical has to be put on hold, then that's a decision you'll have to make. Seeking new horizons becomes more important as the year advances.

8 TUESDAY *Moon Age Day 8 Moon Sign Cancer*

Personal matters could be slightly up in the air right now, and it's even more important that you look at all situations fairly and with the even-handed approach for which you are justifiably famous. Any sort of family gathering could suit you at present, as would travel that is arranged at the last minute.

9 WEDNESDAY *Moon Age Day 9 Moon Sign Leo*

There's always a danger that frustrations at work might lead to disputes, but arguing is not really your way and doesn't achieve much for the steady sign of Libra. Your best approach is to stay on the outside of disagreements when you can and make it plain that you won't take sides. Of course, this might make you unpopular with both sides!

10 THURSDAY *Moon Age Day 10 Moon Sign Leo*

Offering help to friends is the name of the game today, and you ought to be showing the most sympathetic and positive side of your nature in personal matters. If you realise your partner needs your support, you should be quite ready to do almost anything necessary to make them happy. It's time to demonstrate how active and enterprising Libra can be.

11 FRIDAY *Moon Age Day 11 Moon Sign Virgo*

Be prepared to deal with financial setbacks. This could mean being more careful about what you are spending, though if you keep your eyes open you should still have scope to secure a bargain. Make the most of opportunities to bring people back into your life, particularly those who have been absent for quite some time.

12 SATURDAY *Moon Age Day 12 Moon Sign Virgo*

Changes in family situations might mean having to alter your perspectives somewhat. Younger family members especially could benefit greatly from your common-sense approach to life. Approaching them with care is the best way to persuade them to listen. Motivation is the key for Libra now, with personal matters being the main beneficiary.

13 SUNDAY *Moon Age Day 13 Moon Sign Virgo*

It pays to put patient effort into getting organised this Sunday, both for yourself and on account of family members. Although you want to do the best you can for everyone, there are occasions on which you must please yourself first. It might seem selfish, but it is often the first step towards helping others too.

14 MONDAY *Moon Age Day 14 Moon Sign Libra*

What you really need to appreciate today is how lucky you are. There are gains to be made under the lunar high from taking plans from the past and running with them. You can make the most of the assistance on offer, as well as putting your own personal slant on life. In any situation it is worth committing yourself fully.

15 TUESDAY *Moon Age Day 15 Moon Sign Libra*

You now have all the energy you could need in order to accomplish some of your personal goals. There should be help around if you need it, though there's nothing wrong with choosing to rely almost entirely on yourself. This doesn't necessarily mean that you have to ignore those around you, because sociability can bring its own rewards.

16 WEDNESDAY *Moon Age Day 16 Moon Sign Scorpio*

A total change of scenery would be a positive step today, though it might require you to relinquish control of something, at least temporarily. You have what it takes to make fun not only for yourself but for a host of other people too. Concentrate on putting right anything that is proving to be an irritation in your love life.

17 THURSDAY *Moon Age Day 17 Moon Sign Scorpio*

Though independence could seem quite appealing at the present time, you probably can't expect to please yourself all the time today. You live in a world filled with other people, most of whom have a definite point of view of their own. Where your life meshes with those of others you have little choice but to look for compromises.

18 FRIDAY *Moon Age Day 18 Moon Sign Sagittarius*

Capitalising on today's opportunities means filling up your social diary and enjoying life in the company of people you find stimulating and interesting. Not everyone is good to know – but that's life! Stay the course in new ventures and do your best in competitive activities. Even if you don't win, it's worth taking part.

19 SATURDAY *Moon Age Day 19 Moon Sign Sagittarius*

This has potential to be a positive period generally and especially so for Libran people who work during the weekend. If you don't, then concentrate instead on having a good time. With plenty to play for in a social sense, you might also decide to simplify your romantic life somewhat in order to make things more comfortable.

20 SUNDAY *Moon Age Day 20 Moon Sign Sagittarius*

Look ahead to new beginnings in social matters. If you're willing to be a team player you should be able to get on well with just about everyone, and can easily modify your own nature to suit whatever is going on around you. Private conversations can help you to glean some interesting information, maybe about future travel plans.

21 MONDAY *Moon Age Day 21 Moon Sign Capricorn*

Make the most of an element of luck that is on offer in career developments around now. Having said that, much of what is happening is down to your own effort across a considerable period of time. Don't be too quick to believe everything you are told, especially by anyone who might have a vested interest in soft-soap.

22 TUESDAY *Moon Age Day 22 Moon Sign Capricorn*

Anything that you feel is not succeeding in the outside world is probably best ignored for the moment, in favour of tackling what you know is working well for you. Beware of getting involved in get-rich-quick schemes, because they rarely work out. Rock-solid investments work best for you now, in terms of both time and money.

23 WEDNESDAY *Moon Age Day 23 Moon Sign Aquarius*

Slight problems are a distinct possibility when it comes to financial matters, and keeping your money firmly locked into your purse or wallet would be no bad thing. There's a time for spending and a period when it is best to save, and you are right in the middle of the latter during this midweek period. Controlling your outgoings is the name of the game.

24 THURSDAY *Moon Age Day 24 Moon Sign Aquarius*

Now is a favourable time to make strides forward with regard to your long-term ambitions. There are gains to be made from simply talking to the right people, and from pursuing ideas that you have had for some time. Family matters are well accented, and it's important to register the joy and pride you feel about those who are close to you.

25 FRIDAY *Moon Age Day 25 Moon Sign Pisces*

The signs are that today might not be the best day of the month when it comes to your love life. Success in this area depends on the attitude of those involved, and if something is amiss, it will be difficult to find fulfilment. For this reason you may decide to stick with friends today because there is more to be gained in a general sense.

26 SATURDAY *Moon Age Day 26 Moon Sign Pisces*

Sudden tensions could now arise in your life, and you should be doing everything you can to avoid these. Are these caused by the attitudes and opinions of others? If so, one option is to simply ignore them. Stick with friends you know well and especially people who are not cynical or critical.

27 SUNDAY *Moon Age Day 27 Moon Sign Aries*

Be aware of any risks you are taking because the lunar low is not an ideal time to be taking a gamble, especially in terms of cash. Today is about sticking to what you know and keeping life as moderate as possible. Of course, other people may be more reactive and inclined to fly off the handle for no real reason!

28 MONDAY *Moon Age Day 28 Moon Sign Aries*

Socially speaking this may not be the easiest time, but the fact is that astrological trends are doing little to assist you today. That doesn't mean you should hide in a corner, because that clearly isn't your style around now, though you may feel the need for a little seclusion. For now there's nothing wrong with being happy with your own company.

29 TUESDAY *Moon Age Day 29 Moon Sign Taurus*

Even if professional interests are of paramount importance at present, you should still be able to find time to look at both romance and friendship. Do you feel a little let down by the way certain people have been behaving of late? If so, you need to recognise that they may well have your best interests at heart.

30 WEDNESDAY *Moon Age Day 0 Moon Sign Taurus*

While some of your ambitions might tail off for a short time under current influences, you shouldn't lack enthusiasm when you are doing something you really like. However, there's always a risk that you'll be tempted to do too many things at once. Concentrate on the task in hand and make sure you succeed before moving on.

May 2014

1 THURSDAY *Moon Age Day 1 Moon Sign Gemini*

It's the first day of May, and capitalising on social opportunities is just what the doctor ordered for you at this time. Today is about registering the pull of the season, and about your desire to be involved in a whole range of activities. You have what it takes to succeed at something that has been a problem in the past.

2 FRIDAY *Moon Age Day 2 Moon Sign Gemini*

This is a favourable time for revitalising elements of your personal life. Focusing on emotional issues would be no bad thing, though that does bring the possibility of disagreements from within romantic attachments. Trends encourage contact with people who either live at a distance or you simply don't see very often.

3 SATURDAY *Moon Age Day 3 Moon Sign Gemini*

Disputes are a distinct possibility, even if you are not the one creating them or even directly involved. You can be the world's natural diplomat, but you do need to be careful that you avoid being seen as an antagonist. One of your options is simply to stay away from warring parties altogether.

4 SUNDAY *Moon Age Day 4 Moon Sign Cancer*

Problems and obstacles can be overcome if you are willing to apply a combination of common sense and intuition. Working out the way others are likely to behave under any given circumstance should help you to make progress, and this is also a time to find ways of contributing to the success of specific family members.

5 MONDAY *Moon Age Day 5 Moon Sign Cancer*

Professional challenges are indicated for the start of the working week, and you need to take these in your stride as surely as anything else that seems to take effort. With a real sense of urgency you now have scope to break down any red tape that surrounds you and get to the heart of matters when you need to. Seek help from friends.

6 TUESDAY *Moon Age Day 6 Moon Sign Leo*

Be prepared to respond to challenges from others in a professional sense, though you needn't allow these to throw you off course. You can't bank on everything going your way under present astrological influences. The important thing is that you use all your energy and determination to get you to the winning post.

7 WEDNESDAY *Moon Age Day 7 Moon Sign Leo*

You have scope to enjoy a special time with someone you love a great deal. This is one of the most auspicious days of the month for romance, and offers you the chance to really find exactly the right words. Be ready to deal with potentially embarrassing situations arising from any unexpected expressions of emotion.

8 THURSDAY *Moon Age Day 8 Moon Sign Leo*

Much energy can now be channelled into fulfilling some of your ambitions, especially in a professional and practical sense. There should be time for simple enjoyment later in the day, and it is important that you don't spend all day concentrating. Relaxation is the name of the game by the time the evening comes along.

9 FRIDAY *Moon Age Day 9 Moon Sign Virgo*

The spotlight is now on your ability to interact with others and to understand how their minds are working. This sort of deep intuition is typical of your zodiac sign and it can be somewhat uncomfortable on occasions because your empathy is so complete. It's worth remembering that you have your own life to live too.

10 SATURDAY *Moon Age Day 10 Moon Sign Virgo*

Even if you feel your powers are somewhat limited at this time, you needn't allow this fact to get in the way too much. For today a twelfth-house Moon dominates, and it will take an extra burst of effort on your part to get where you really want to be. One option is to avoid professional matters and stick to enjoying yourself.

11 SUNDAY *Moon Age Day 11 Moon Sign Libra*

The arrival of the lunar high offers you one of the best days of the month for starting new projects. With plenty of enthusiasm and the greatest determination possible to succeed, what is likely to stand in your way? Avoid unnecessary routines and stick to the task in hand because you wouldn't want to waste a moment of these positive trends.

12 MONDAY *Moon Age Day 12 Moon Sign Libra*

Personal triumphs of one sort or another are now within your reach. Even if these don't appear to be very significant at first, you should be able to recognise their implications before very long. It pays to keep up the cheerful front you put in place a while ago. It is now far less difficult for you to believe it is real.

13 TUESDAY *Moon Age Day 13 Moon Sign Libra*

The lunar high continues, offering another day on which you should be ready for action and keen to get ahead. If you haven't done so already, you need to ensure that any lingering negatives disappear like the morning mist, leaving you in the right frame of mind to really get ahead. You can persuade the whole world to love you now!

14 WEDNESDAY *Moon Age Day 14 Moon Sign Scorpio*

It's natural to feel rather suspicious of the motives of certain other people, and that can make for a slightly uncomfortable day in some respects. It would be best to give them the benefit of the doubt, though that doesn't mean surrendering your control altogether. In some respects you might be slightly over-cautious.

Visited M & D as usual – Dad very tired.

15 THURSDAY *Moon Age Day 15 Moon Sign Scorpio*

This is a fortuitous interlude for spending time with others, and it's important to capitalise on the positive trends that presently surround you. You have everything you need in order to give a good impression and to boost your popularity. If there is something you want but you have been afraid to ask for it, this would be an ideal period to have a go.

pm I pack for stay at M & D's for D to get some sleep.

16 FRIDAY *Moon Age Day 16 Moon Sign Sagittarius*

Be on the look-out for the new and the unusual in almost anything (1) you undertake at the moment, as this could assist you to stretch credibility on a number of different occasions. Rather than arguing for your limitations, why not believe yourself to be capable of anything? You won't be – but it's a start!

I go to M & D's for overnight stay No. 2

17 SATURDAY *Moon Age Day 17 Moon Sign Sagittarius*

This is a day during which you need to focus on the practical side (2) of life. This means rolling up your sleeves and getting stuck in, alongside others who clearly have your best interests at heart as well as their own. Be ready to make the final push in a low-key battle you have been fighting for some time, if the opportunity arises.

I go to M & D's for overnight stay No. 3

18 SUNDAY *Moon Age Day 18 Moon Sign Capricorn*

Trends assist you to attend to several different jobs at the same time (3) today and still manage to do them all justice. That's not especially unusual for Libra, though you do sometimes push yourself a little too hard. There ought to be the opportunity around now to take some sort of interesting break, so take advantage of this.

I put my light out at 1.50 am !!

19 MONDAY *Moon Age Day 19 Moon Sign Capricorn*

Personal concerns and domestic duties are particularly emphasised right now. It is possible that they will distract you from obligations elsewhere, but as long as you make the necessary apologies you can deal with these later. What can really make the difference today is not rushing things or overcrowding your schedule.

20 TUESDAY *Moon Age Day 20 Moon Sign Aquarius*

If there are still any minor obstacles around, you should be in a position to deal with them quickly and efficiently. It pays to get your skates on today if you want to get something done ahead of the competition. Your ability to think and act quickly is now to the fore, so there shouldn't be any difficulty about your ultimate success.

21 WEDNESDAY *Moon Age Day 21 Moon Sign Aquarius*

While your personal and emotional life is well accented now, the same cannot be said for family attachments, in which an element of strain is possible. Even if problems aren't your fault, it's up to you to apply a great deal of patience. It should be worthwhile in the end, especially if you can see that your attitude is appreciated.

22 THURSDAY *Moon Age Day 22 Moon Sign Pisces*

Communication matters are the best area of life for you now, no matter what sphere of your life is involved. Don't keep quiet when you know it is necessary to speak out, and be willing to act in a moment to protect your own interests. There may be less awkwardness around at home, though there are good reasons to monitor the situation.

23 FRIDAY *Moon Age Day 23 Moon Sign Pisces*

This could be a make-or-break time in terms of some facets of your life. There are always going to be a few people who are difficult to deal with, but you are now equipped to take such matters in your stride. When you have to make decisions, keep everyone informed by all means, but do what you think is right in the end.

24 SATURDAY *Moon Age Day 24 Moon Sign Aries*

Extra work seems to be the order of today, but what is really happening is that the arrival of the lunar low can put a rather negative gloss on things. Your best approach is to allow others to take some of the strain and not to be too quick off the mark with new schemes. You might even decide to leave significant plans until after Sunday.

25 SUNDAY *Moon Age Day 25 Moon Sign Aries*

Slacken the pace now and be willing to watch and wait. You can make this a positive day, despite the lunar low, if you simply settle for what is on offer. There is much to be said for adopting a slightly quieter approach than usual, which could be a surprise to others. That needn't stop you remaining optimistic, though still happy to wait a while.

26 MONDAY *Moon Age Day 26 Moon Sign Taurus*

Social and teamwork efforts work best for you now, particularly if you manage to clear the fog of yesterday. You are fairly sure what you want from life and should have a good idea about how you are going to get it. Think twice before agreeing to anything that is going to mean a great deal of work for very little reward.

27 TUESDAY *Moon Age Day 27 Moon Sign Taurus*

Love life involvements can sometimes seem to be more trouble than they are worth, and that could well be the case at the moment. It's important to consider your partner's state of mind, and to take this into account when deciding what to do. Patience is the key, because things should settle down in time.

28 WEDNESDAY *Moon Age Day 28 Moon Sign Taurus*

The charismatic side of your nature is to the fore at the moment, assisting you to approach life pretty much as would be expected of Libra. This is an ideal opportunity to focus on travel plans, and if you are seeking advancement at work, but not succeeding, now is the time to take your courage in your own hands and ask.

29 THURSDAY *Moon Age Day 0 Moon Sign Gemini*

Current trends favour all information gathering, and it is quite possible for you to get ahead by simply being in the right place at the most advantageous time. Romance looks more settled, and you can ensure this continues by being aware of your partner's attitude. If your relationship has just started, it pays to get off on the right foot.

30 FRIDAY *Moon Age Day 1 Moon Sign Gemini*

Take full advantage of the chance to assess how well certain plans are maturing. If they aren't moving at all, now is the period to think up new strategies. There are gains to be made by clearing the decks for action in a number of different ways, though your attention should be focused on the medium and long term rather than the next few days.

31 SATURDAY *Moon Age Day 2 Moon Sign Cancer*

There are good reasons to seek a complete change of scenery if you can this weekend, and if you can persuade others to keep you company along the way, so much the better. Libra is not usually a solo player, and especially not right now. Exciting new social developments may be available soon, so it's worthwhile keeping your eyes open.

June

2014

1 SUNDAY *Moon Age Day 3 Moon Sign Cancer*

The emphasis today is on ensuring that others don't get hold of the wrong end of the stick, at least as far as your comments are concerned. Be prepared to explain yourself fully and make sure that others understand you. This doesn't necessarily mean that the day is gloom and doom. On the contrary, it has some really positive social and personal potential.

2 MONDAY *Moon Age Day 4 Moon Sign Cancer*

Domestic and family influences have a powerful part to play in your thinking at the start of this week, and you may be slightly overtaken by events of a more personal nature. Romance is certainly there for the taking for many Librans. It appears that not only nature is waking up at this time of year, so are you!

3 TUESDAY *Moon Age Day 5 Moon Sign Leo*

A happy-go-lucky phase is indicated right now, encouraging you to show a real zest for living that is certain to be infectious. Today's trends are favourable for educational matters and for getting to grips with anything you haven't altogether understood. Why not seek out a little advice from someone who is older or wiser?

4 WEDNESDAY *Moon Age Day 6 Moon Sign Leo*

Social connections are now very useful and can assist you to mix business with pleasure. There is nothing wrong with feathering your own nest, particularly if you are also willing to keep an eye out for others on the way. Showing colleagues how confident you are might even convince them to emulate your actions.

5 THURSDAY *Moon Age Day 7 Moon Sign Virgo*

Be ready to deal with moments of high drama in relationships. Even if these are caused by others rather than by anything you are doing, you might still need to react to them. Your interests are best served by taking things seriously, even if you find them ridiculous. Show that Libran patience and talk things through, especially with your partner.

6 FRIDAY *Moon Age Day 8 Moon Sign Virgo*

Look for opportunities to cultivate anyone who is in a position of authority today. Adopt your best and most charming attitude and you will be amazed how far you can go. Not only can you persuade others to do things for you, they might even fall over themselves to do so! Be willing to help friends who need your support, especially later on.

7 SATURDAY ☿ *Moon Age Day 9 Moon Sign Virgo*

You can afford to take some time to yourself this weekend. Everything is set fair in terms of your professional life, but unless you work during the weekend this is unlikely to be of any use. Better instead to spend time with those you love, as well as looking carefully at the needs of the people who are closest to you.

8 SUNDAY ☿ *Moon Age Day 10 Moon Sign Libra*

The lunar high is definitely the best time of the month to put new ideas to the test. There's everything to play for and many situations that you can turn to your advantage. Routines are for the birds now, because your focus should be on pleasing yourself and breaking down barriers as often as you can.

9 MONDAY ☿ *Moon Age Day 11 Moon Sign Libra*

The presence of the lunar high allows you to clear your mind and makes it possible for you to see right through to the heart of any situation. That doesn't mean you have to spend your time waiting around. On the contrary, this ought to be a day of action. It doesn't much matter what you decide to do, simply that you ensure it's enjoyable.

10 TUESDAY ☿ *Moon Age Day 12 Moon Sign Scorpio*

You have scope to gain plenty of inspiration now through social activities of one sort or another. Even if you are busy from a practical and professional point of view, there's nothing to stop you from taking time out. This is just as well, because all work and no play tends to make Libra a less than happy individual.

11 WEDNESDAY ☿ *Moon Age Day 13 Moon Sign Scorpio*

When it comes to getting the edge in any sort of business association, the trends definitely assist you now. What you might lack is a killer instinct, though the people around you would probably consider this to be a very good thing. It's up to you to find ways and means of advancing, but not at the expense of your colleagues.

12 THURSDAY ☿ *Moon Age Day 14 Moon Sign Sagittarius*

You can have a great deal of influence when it comes to financial progress at this stage of the working week. Not only this, but your ability to assess situations immediately is particularly highlighted. It's time to show what a good friend you can be, perhaps by doing what you can to help someone out of a pickle.

13 FRIDAY ☿ *Moon Age Day 15 Moon Sign Sagittarius*

This would be a very good time during which to clear the air in a family sense. You have what it takes to settle any disputes once and for all, and can even use your skills to deal with wayward types who have been inconsiderate recently. Even if life isn't plain sailing, you can at least make sure it's interesting.

14 SATURDAY ☿ *Moon Age Day 16 Moon Sign Capricorn*

Changes and emotional confrontations are indicated, so much so that this could turn out to be a very surprising day. You need to bear in mind that not everything that looks unfortunate turns out to be so, and you have a chance to discover a great deal about yourself as a result of your instinctive reactions today. Why not opt for a social sort of evening?

15 SUNDAY ☿ *Moon Age Day 17 Moon Sign Capricorn*

Stand up for yourself in discussions by all means, but avoid allowing these to degenerate into arguments. For one thing, there isn't time to be at odds with anyone if you are to capitalise on what can be an eventful and potentially interesting day. It's worth using a little psychology with family members because this can work better than domination now.

16 MONDAY ☿ *Moon Age Day 18 Moon Sign Aquarius*

There are good reasons to concentrate on material wealth, and current trends assist you to find ways to increase your financial wherewithal. The time is right to seek out new avenues and to take on board the very good advice that you can glean from both colleagues and friends. By the evening you can turn your attention towards romance.

17 TUESDAY ☿ *Moon Age Day 19 Moon Sign Aquarius*

Your love life and romantic matters are now well marked, so this would be an ideal time to find ways of making your partner happy, or to set up an interesting date if you don't have a partner at the moment. Coming up with the right words to sweep someone off their feet is easier for most Libran people than they think.

18 WEDNESDAY ☿ *Moon Age Day 20 Moon Sign Pisces*

Patience is the order of the day in any really trying situations to do with love at the moment. Don't expect sweetness and light coming from everyone, because that is unrealistic at present. Rather than being depressed about the fact, you need to realise that you have the power now to turn almost any situation around.

19 THURSDAY ☿ *Moon Age Day 21 Moon Sign Pisces*

A vital decision you take now could help you to achieve a profitable result later, but which way to jump? Only you can decide, using a combination of knowledge and intuition. Listen to the little voice at the back of your mind in any situation you are not sure about. Be prepared to approach friends for help, but don't ignore their entertainment value!

20 FRIDAY ☿ *Moon Age Day 22 Moon Sign Aries*

Tackling even the simplest tasks can be fraught with frustration today. The lunar low takes the shine off any luck that is available, or at least that may be the way it seems from your point of view. Remember that this is nothing more than a temporary interlude, and get on with matters that don't need too much concentration.

21 SATURDAY ☿ *Moon Age Day 23 Moon Sign Aries*

Beware of jumping to conclusions about others. It's tempting to go on your gut feelings, but if you don't collect enough evidence there's a risk that your judgements will be unsound. Take your time and get back into the mainstream of life slowly. As the day wears on you ought to be ready to display more confidence and energy.

22 SUNDAY ☿ *Moon Age Day 24 Moon Sign Aries*

Your wanderlust is highlighted now, which isn't entirely unusual for Libra and certainly not at this time of year. Make the best of any good weather that's around by getting away from the ordinary routines of everyday life. You might even decide to extend the weekend by taking a day off work tomorrow, and that would suit present trends fine.

23 MONDAY ☿ *Moon Age Day 25 Moon Sign Taurus*

If you begin to think big you stand more chance of convincing other people of your personal power. That doesn't mean you should be lording it over anyone. Today is about proving you are good to know and that you will do almost anything to please others. This is Libra at its best, and helps you to make this a generally happy and contented day.

24 TUESDAY ☿ *Moon Age Day 26 Moon Sign Taurus*

There could now be a slight downside to personal attachments, particularly if you are not choosing your words carefully or saying exactly the right thing. You need to be very specific and to lay on the compliments with a trowel if you want to avoid contentious situations. It might not be fair – but it is life.

25 WEDNESDAY ☿ *Moon Age Day 27 Moon Sign Gemini*

An ideal day to put your considerable energy into money-making projects, though socialising is less favoured, at least until tomorrow. Your powers of concentration count for a great deal, and you should be using these to your best advantage. If confidence is lacking somewhat, it's worth seeking some compliments and support at some stage today.

26 THURSDAY ☿ *Moon Age Day 28 Moon Sign Gemini*

Financial matters show great promise of gain, and it's also time to demonstrate your ability to succeed at work right now. If you are between positions at the moment this would be an ideal interlude to concentrate all those efforts. Someone, somewhere, can't do without your unique talents. You just have to find out who they are!

27 FRIDAY ☿ *Moon Age Day 0 Moon Sign Cancer*

A socially helpful period is now at hand and along comes a Friday during which you can afford to let the practical side of life take a definite back seat. The emphasis today is on your ability to enjoy yourself and to help others do the same. Life can be all smiles, but it is important not to leave anyone out if you can avoid doing so.

28 SATURDAY ☿ *Moon Age Day 1 Moon Sign Cancer*

It's up to you to capitalise on the good fortune that is now on offer. It's possible you will want to make improvements at home, and domestic matters are certainly to the fore throughout much of the week ahead. Any sort of change to your environment can be beneficial, as long as you make sure you're in the swing of what's going on.

29 SUNDAY ☿ *Moon Age Day 2 Moon Sign Cancer*

Trends suggest this may not be the best day for decision-making, particularly if you have plenty to do and don't want to spend time considering pros and cons. One option is to get as far away from mundane life as you can and treat yourself to a dose of make-believe. If you can do it in the company of someone you care for – even better.

30 MONDAY ☿ *Moon Age Day 3 Moon Sign Leo*

If others find you to be rather too assertive for their liking, isn't that really their problem? Rather than turning down the volume, you need to recognise that you can't please everyone, and that some might like you just the way you are. Justifiable criticism is fine, but envy is another thing entirely. Be proud of the sort of person you are.

July 2014

1 TUESDAY ☿ *Moon Age Day 4 Moon Sign Leo*

Review past efforts for the best chance of getting ahead right now. Contributing to your own eventual success is possible, but it'll be tricky to get everything you want without relying on others more than has been the case recently. Confidence is well accented in some areas, though it could be distinctly lacking in others.

2 WEDNESDAY *Moon Age Day 5 Moon Sign Virgo*

You have what it takes to keep romantic matters settled and interesting, and to get the most pleasure from this area of life out here in the middle of the week. It's a matter of ensuring you say all the right things, and making the most of the compliments you can attract from others. Avoid spending money when it isn't necessary to do so.

3 THURSDAY *Moon Age Day 6 Moon Sign Virgo*

It's important at the moment to listen to any messages that are coming from those who are special to you. This might be a slightly frustrating day in one way or another, particularly if you feel that the people you rely on a professional sense are not performing to the best of their ability. Attitude is the key to making progress in practical matters.

4 FRIDAY *Moon Age Day 7 Moon Sign Virgo*

Be prepared to welcome personalities into your life around now, and take advantage of all the opportunities they make available to you. Attitude is very important today because if you show the world at large that you know what you are doing and that you are trustworthy, you are well on the way to being able to achieve almost anything.

5 SATURDAY *Moon Age Day 8 Moon Sign Libra*

The arrival of the lunar high heralds a winning streak, and there isn't much that stands beyond your power to control. It's time to put any bashfulness to one side, and to make sure all eyes are on you. Capitalising on these trends allows you to star in any role you create for yourself. Life can be a ball for Librans who take the initiative now.

6 SUNDAY *Moon Age Day 9 Moon Sign Libra*

Success today is about putting your practical thoughts into words that the world understands. In addition, it's important to register the activities of your friends and your relatives, particularly if they are actively seeking you out. Stay away from situations over which you can have no influence and which might prove awkward.

7 MONDAY *Moon Age Day 10 Moon Sign Scorpio*

Present trends can help you to find solutions to any problems that have been a bind for some time. The spotlight is on your clear-thinking approach and your ability to get to the heart of any matter almost instantly. Others might be envious of this talent, so don't be surprised if they decide to pick your brains when it best suits their purposes.

8 TUESDAY *Moon Age Day 11 Moon Sign Scorpio*

Those higher up the professional tree than you are might prove to be especially useful at the moment, but this does depend on your own attitude, which needs to be positive and helpful. Once again, personalities have a part to play in your life around now, and it's important to take account of the interesting changes of direction they present.

9 WEDNESDAY *Moon Age Day 12 Moon Sign Scorpio*

Challenges and career moves should be easy to deal with, and this is a time during which you can afford to take on new responsibilities. It pays to show how impressive you can be when in company, and this can assist you to attract some significant compliments. Present trends are also favourable when it comes to love and romance.

10 THURSDAY *Moon Age Day 13 Moon Sign Sagittarius*

Most friendship issues are positively highlighted, and it ought to be a piece of cake to persuade others to do your bidding. That doesn't mean you have to be selfish, especially if you ensure that your present intentions suit others as much as they do you. This has potential to be a socially rewarding day, with plenty of romantic possibilities too.

11 FRIDAY *Moon Age Day 14 Moon Sign Sagittarius*

Professional circles offer opportunities for new friendships and new ways of looking at old situations. What can make all the difference at the moment is your ability to cut through red tape and get to the heart of any matter. If you can convince other people to follow your lead, there should be little to stop you putting a few plans into action.

12 SATURDAY *Moon Age Day 15 Moon Sign Capricorn*

Even if you feel that your emotional security is being threatened in some way, you need to avoid hanging on to the past. Instead, your best approach is to project your mind forward and make slow and steady progress. Anything old could be of particular interest to you at the moment, so visiting art galleries or museums would be one option.

13 SUNDAY *Moon Age Day 16 Moon Sign Capricorn*

It could prove profitable now to speak your mind. If you do so diplomatically you stand the best chance of being listened to carefully, especially by superiors. By all means stand by decisions you have made, even if this means working harder than usual, but you also need to understand that flexibility can be a distinct boon.

14 MONDAY *Moon Age Day 17 Moon Sign Aquarius*

Capitalise on the positive attention you can now attract from friends, and on the opportunities you have to make some new pals. New interests are the order of the day, and it's up to you to find plenty of things to do. Your charm is well accented under current influences, which should help you to get what you most want.

St Swithin's Day.

15 TUESDAY *Moon Age Day 18 Moon Sign Aquarius*

There are good reasons to quicken the pace of life now, and even if others fall by the wayside, you ought to be able to keep up. Focus your attention where it is needed the most and be willing to change horses in midstream if it proves to be necessary. Nobody is more on the ball than you at present – but you do need to show it!

16 WEDNESDAY *Moon Age Day 19 Moon Sign Pisces*

You shouldn't be short of good ideas today because this can be one of the most inspired periods you are likely to have during July. It certainly pays to keep abreast of the news in the area where you live. However, it would be sensible to make certain you really understand particular issues before getting too deeply involved.

17 THURSDAY *Moon Age Day 20 Moon Sign Pisces*

Stand by to make the most of a really positive day, but be aware that you'll need to put in plenty of effort if you are to make significant progress. Dashing about from pillar to post is fine, though it might mean you can't spend as much time with loved ones as you wish. Explaining yourself should help to limit the damage.

18 FRIDAY *Moon Age Day 21 Moon Sign Aries*

This would not be a sensible time for struggling against the odds. On the contrary, if you are willing to sit and wait, you stand the best chance of achieving things in the long run. This isn't an attitude that typifies Libra in a general sense, but while the lunar low is around there may be little point in knocking your head against a wall.

19 SATURDAY *Moon Age Day 22 Moon Sign Aries*

Progress may be rather slow right now whilst the lunar low is around, so much so that your best approach is to stick to thinking rather than doing. This is not an ideal time for taking on anything new, and it's worth postponing any plans you have to push the bounds of the possible until early next week.

20 SUNDAY *Moon Age Day 23 Moon Sign Taurus*

Sympathetic trends now surround family associations, encouraging you to actively choose to spend time with your nearest and dearest. Today is excellent for entertaining at home and for making sure that friends are happy and content. The signs are that Libra wants to be everywhere at the moment, but works best from a sound domestic base.

21 MONDAY *Moon Age Day 24 Moon Sign Taurus*

This could prove to be an especially good time with regard to goals and objectives. Financial security also comes under the spotlight, and there is much to be said for seeking ways to improve money matters. Look out for opportunities up ahead to do some sort of deal that offsets previous monetary hiccups.

22 TUESDAY *Moon Age Day 25 Moon Sign Gemini*

Despite a few potential challenges, professional matters hold greater potential for you today than they have done for a couple of weeks. That doesn't mean you have to concentrate solely on this area of your life. On the contrary, there should also be an emphasis on fun and on joining in with any shindig that is taking place.

23 WEDNESDAY *Moon Age Day 26 Moon Sign Gemini*

Monetary gains are the name of the game, and this would be a favourable interlude to find ways of improving family finances. Be prepared for some embarrassment if you decide you need to tell specific individuals some home truths. That needn't stop you ending the day with something very entertaining, utterly decadent and far too expensive!

24 THURSDAY *Moon Age Day 27 Moon Sign Gemini*

It's natural to be concerned about the welfare of loved ones right now, though you need to ask yourself whether there is actually any real justification for this. Your best approach is to look at situations quite carefully before you start worrying about them. The day can certainly be improved if you are willing to stop, get your breath and start again slowly.

25 FRIDAY

Moon Age Day 28 Moon Sign Cancer

A new focus on money is indicated, accompanied by a 'me and mine' attitude on your part that is unusual for Libra. You have what it takes to strengthen your financial position, though it could mean being a bit more mercenary than has been the case of late. Understanding the behaviour of all those around you might be tricky at the moment.

26 SATURDAY

Moon Age Day 29 Moon Sign Cancer

Look out for encouraging news now, and be ready to reap rewards from short trips. It's worth seeking out people you don't see very often, and you need to make the best of a day on which there might not be much time to concentrate on professional or practical matters. Why not treat today as a holiday and persuade others to take the strain?

27 SUNDAY

Moon Age Day 0 Moon Sign Leo

Dwelling on the past is all very well today, though it probably isn't going to be of much help in a general sense. Better by far to commit yourself to the present and the future, and to concentrate on what matters the most to your life as it stands. Nostalgia in fine in its place but is no alternative to simply getting stuck in.

28 MONDAY

Moon Age Day 1 Moon Sign Leo

Around this time you have scope to approach life with great gusto and a determination that is second to none. Even if others are arguing for their own limitations, you need to be committing yourself fully to getting ahead. All matters to do with communication are much enhanced by present planetary positions.

29 TUESDAY

Moon Age Day 2 Moon Sign Leo

Your mental faculties are now emphasised, assisting you to be spot-on with your judgements. It's important that you are much more committed to the future than was the case earlier in the year, and that you are willing to shine, especially in romantic and social situations. It's only Tuesday, though that needn't prevent you from getting into a weekend frame of mind already!

30 WEDNESDAY *Moon Age Day 3 Moon Sign Virgo*

Disputes at home are best avoided, and it pays to stay away from anyone who seems to be very contentious at this time. If you do insist on arguing with anyone, make sure you understand what you are talking about first. You can't expect everyone to be equally helpful today, so you need to think carefully before choosing the company you keep.

31 THURSDAY *Moon Age Day 4 Moon Sign Virgo*

You are encouraged to show improved self-confidence today, and can use this to turn the week in your direction more than might have been the case so far. By tomorrow the lunar high is around again and that is really going to help you pep things up. For now, clear the decks for action and do what you need to prepare for a busier interlude.

August

2014

1 FRIDAY *Moon Age Day 5 Moon Sign Libra*

As the Moon moves back into your zodiac sign, so your influence increases again and you show a marked ability to move forward quickly. The only slight frustration could come if you are not at work today, because the best trends surround professional efforts. All the same, you shouldn't have any trouble filling your time.

2 SATURDAY *Moon Age Day 6 Moon Sign Libra*

This continues to be a really positive interlude for increased influence over life generally, though this being a Saturday it's possible that social matters will predominate over professional ones. What an ideal time this would be to take a journey, even if it's one that is planned at the last minute. Mixing with exciting people can make all the difference.

3 SUNDAY *Moon Age Day 7 Moon Sign Libra*

If there is any reorganising to do at the moment, the lunar high assists you to get into just the right frame of mind to take it on. The results ought to be more than worth the effort, and you are steadily moving towards a new way of looking at old aspects of life. Ask yourself whether you are currently allowing younger relatives enough leeway.

4 MONDAY *Moon Age Day 8 Moon Sign Scorpio*

The signs are that someone you meet today, perhaps in a professional capacity, can have a tremendous bearing on the way your mind is working. This is not a time to stand on ceremony, but a period during which you have to tell the world at large the way you see things. You can be relied upon to use your accustomed diplomacy all the same.

5 TUESDAY *Moon Age Day 9 Moon Sign Scorpio*

Certain tensions are possible at home, particularly in connection with the way a loved one is behaving. There's nothing wrong with offering your point of view, but there may be little else you can do other than to be willing to wait and see. Trends suggest that some of the best moments today are available via friends rather than relatives.

6 WEDNESDAY *Moon Age Day 10 Moon Sign Sagittarius*

There are times within social contacts that you can make a real difference to the way those around you are thinking, and this is particularly true with regard to work colleagues and past associates. You need to recognise that it's possible to be rather too serious for your own good, and to be willing to redress the balance if necessary.

7 THURSDAY *Moon Age Day 11 Moon Sign Sagittarius*

Social matters could now be the source of some promising new developments. It's time to show everyone how friendly you can be, and how much you are willing to share what you have. Although very slight hiccups in romantic attachments can't be ruled out, when it matters the most you can afford to rely on your partner or sweetheart.

8 FRIDAY *Moon Age Day 12 Moon Sign Capricorn*

Your imagination is easily stimulated around now and you shouldn't have any difficulty at all following the possibilities that come about as a result of a daydream. It's natural to want to tackle issues that have been on your mind for some time. However, backing up your case will require plenty of evidence – are you convinced that you have enough?

9 SATURDAY *Moon Age Day 13 Moon Sign Capricorn*

The planetary focus at the moment seems to be quite definitely on the past, and emotional influences could well crop up at this time. Anything that allows you to step out of the limelight can be seen as a positive thing. There's nothing wrong with spending time alone, in a contemplative frame of mind.

10 SUNDAY *Moon Age Day 14 Moon Sign Aquarius*

Try to avoid too much daydreaming at the moment because what really works best today is concrete action. If you find that rules and regulations are getting on your nerves, one option is to spend some time working out how to circumnavigate them altogether. The mischievous side of the Libra nature is highlighted at the moment.

11 MONDAY *Moon Age Day 15 Moon Sign Aquarius*

It's time to find things to celebrate at home, and to make sure this a positive day all round. Confidence shouldn't be lacking when you need it the most, and there are gains to be made by showing your friendliest face to the world at large. This is Libra at its best, and is one of the things that help you to captivate others.

12 TUESDAY *Moon Age Day 16 Moon Sign Pisces*

Exciting social plans can be put on the agenda at this time, and the emphasis is on your determination to have fun. By all means give yourself a pat on the back for any recent successes, but don't allow this to get in the way of your continued efforts to get ahead. Be ready to welcome someone very special into your life around now.

13 WEDNESDAY *Moon Age Day 17 Moon Sign Pisces*

Trends suggest that your imagination might not be quite as well connected to reality today as is usually the case. It's important to bring your powers of discrimination to bear, especially in situations where something looks too good to be true. Your best approach is to be as sceptical as possible around this time.

14 THURSDAY *Moon Age Day 18 Moon Sign Aries*

The lunar low arrives, along with the potential for minor setbacks. As a result, this is not the most auspicious interlude for taking significant chances with life. There's nothing wrong with seeking advice from those you trust and settling for a low-key sort of day, though one that still offers a good deal of potential for personal satisfaction.

15 FRIDAY *Moon Age Day 19 Moon Sign Aries*

You can't expect all objectives to materialise at this time, which is why you need to keep your options well and truly open. If you find the attitude of friends or even relatives difficult to understand today, it's appropriate to ask them to explain themselves. This can make all the difference in terms of your ability to get on side with them.

16 SATURDAY *Moon Age Day 20 Moon Sign Taurus*

A talk with a friend or a colleague can work wonders now. The spotlight is firmly on your plans for a change of job, or maybe for seeking a different sort of responsibility in life altogether. It's time to stretch yourself and to realise that what is actually possible could turn out to be different from what you had imagined.

17 SUNDAY *Moon Age Day 21 Moon Sign Taurus*

You have what it takes to gain from a variety of interests today and from the fact that life is generally on your side. Capitalise on the positive attitudes of those you encounter and look for opportunities to make the best sort of impression on other people. You can't stop family rows from breaking out, but you can choose not to be part of them.

18 MONDAY *Moon Age Day 22 Moon Sign Gemini*

It would be a good idea to concentrate on priorities today before you get sidetracked with all sorts of irrelevant details. Make the most of all new opportunities at work and continue your efforts to create a favourable impression on as many people as possible. Bear in mind that other people do notice you, even if you don't always realise it.

19 TUESDAY *Moon Age Day 23 Moon Sign Gemini*

Make the best of information that comes your way, maybe from colleagues or friends. Others won't always see the potential gains that are at hand, but you need to ensure that you do so. Riding the ups and downs of life is a piece of cake at the moment, and you needn't allow yourself to be swayed once your mind is made up.

20 WEDNESDAY *Moon Age Day 24 Moon Sign Gemini*

Accommodating the needs of others is a natural aspect of life now, though that might mean accepting that you don't have as much time for yourself as you would like. That needn't worry you too much if you feel you are getting a good deal out of life in any case. Don't be too quick to argue for your limitations, especially when it comes to domestic tasks.

21 THURSDAY *Moon Age Day 25 Moon Sign Cancer*

A breezy attitude is the order of the day, and is what allows you to take life fully in your stride. Why not get out of the house and find ways to blow any cobwebs away? You can't expect to get everything you want in a practical sense, so one option is simply to shelve such considerations in favour of finding new ways to have fun.

22 FRIDAY *Moon Age Day 26 Moon Sign Cancer*

Keep abreast of current news and views, particularly at work. It's important that you demonstrate to others that you are interested, even if on occasion you are not. The impression you make on those around you continues to be a key part of your success at the moment, particularly if you are seeking any type of advancement or new responsibilities.

23 SATURDAY *Moon Age Day 27 Moon Sign Leo*

Trends indicate that deep and meaningful attachments have much more to offer you at the moment than casual contacts. If difficulties arise in your dealings with others, ask yourself whether that green-eyed monster jealousy could be part of the reason. You have the ability to make a big impression, but not everyone likes or respects the fact.

24 SUNDAY *Moon Age Day 28 Moon Sign Leo*

Even if you recognise that there is happiness and comfort to be found in family situations, you may decide that this is the last thing you want as you plunge into just about any excitement you can think of. Being told what to do is unlikely to appeal under current planetary influences. There are times when Libra simply wants to please itself.

25 MONDAY *Moon Age Day 0 Moon Sign Leo*

The domestic scene needs a positive approach now, and your ability to listen very carefully to what family members are saying can make all the difference. This is even more vital if your partner has some axe to grind. There are some situations you can't do much about, but what really matters is your willingness to at least lend an ear.

26 TUESDAY *Moon Age Day 1 Moon Sign Virgo*

You have what it takes to benefit from more personal freedom now, and that means making the most of life. It is quality that matters today, rather than quantity, and so whatever you do, it's worth doing it to the best of your ability. Be ready to offer congratulations to those close to you if the circumstances require it.

27 WEDNESDAY *Moon Age Day 2 Moon Sign Virgo*

Activities on a practical level count for a great deal now, and you can afford to allow the sometimes dreamy side of your nature to take a break. You know what you want from life and in most cases will have a very good idea how to get it. Creative potential is not as good as it might be, but you can't have everything.

28 THURSDAY *Moon Age Day 3 Moon Sign Libra*

With the arrival of the lunar high comes an interlude that is well suited to communicating your personal desires, and if you search for the right words you will probably get somewhere near your objectives. That doesn't mean you can't maintain a thoughtful approach, though that needn't prevent you from seeking opportunities to simply have fun.

29 FRIDAY *Moon Age Day 4 Moon Sign Libra*

This is the time of the month for big thinking and not at all the sort of period during which you should hide your light under a bushel. There are gains to be made in expected and unexpected directions, and this is definitely an interlude during which you need to keep your eyes open. Don't be afraid to act quickly now.

30 SATURDAY *Moon Age Day 5 Moon Sign Libra*

Capitalise on opportunities to win friends and to influence people generally. It's a question of making progress when it is available and seeing openings that others do not. Confidence is definitely to the fore, and you have what it takes to get ahead. Part of this could be suggesting better ways of doing things.

31 SUNDAY *Moon Age Day 6 Moon Sign Scorpio*

Making practical progress is now partly down to how far you can persuade others to work on your behalf. The choice is yours, because it's not certain that everyone concerned is a person you care for very much. There is a time for honesty, even if this leaves you struggling, and a time for telling the odd white lie, which enables you to move forwards.

September

2014

1 MONDAY *Moon Age Day 7 Moon Sign Scorpio*

Communicating your ideas to others shouldn't be difficult now, whether you are dealing with bosses, colleagues or friends. On the romantic front you need to find the right words to express your feelings, and shouldn't rule out using a touch of poetry. If you feel frustrated at younger family members, bear in mind that this might just what they are looking for!

2 TUESDAY *Moon Age Day 8 Moon Sign Sagittarius*

Travel and communication are both extremely well highlighted at the moment, making this an ideal period to get out there and have a good time. Anyone who has chosen this time for a holiday is fortunate indeed. There are good reasons to seek out company that is entertaining, made up of people who have the ability to make you laugh.

3 WEDNESDAY *Moon Age Day 9 Moon Sign Sagittarius*

Planetary trends indicate that you have scope to make progress in social and co-operative ventures at the moment. If there are issues to resolve early in the day, make sure it isn't too long before you are working to the best of your ability and solving a few other problems along the way.

4 THURSDAY *Moon Age Day 10 Moon Sign Capricorn*

A lift to your spirits is available today, assisting you to make the most of some strong social highlights. Arrangements that are made by friends could assist you to create some really interesting interludes, though it is possible that some of these won't actually arrive for a few days. Use today for clearing practical tasks.

5 FRIDAY *Moon Age Day 11 Moon Sign Capricorn*

Beware of becoming over-idealistic about a romantic issue. It is possible that you are not seeing things quite as clearly now as would usually be the case, and there is much to be said for seeking some impartial advice from a friend. The current interlude works best if you ensure that your expectations of life are fairly realistic.

6 SATURDAY *Moon Age Day 12 Moon Sign Aquarius*

Trends highlight the assertive and even somewhat pushy side of your nature at the moment, a fact that could come as a definite surprise to your nearest and dearest. Libra doesn't often display these traits, so it can be rather unsettling for others on those rare occasions when you do.

7 SUNDAY *Moon Age Day 13 Moon Sign Aquarius*

A slight tendency to see things through rose-coloured glasses is the legacy of the present position of the Sun, and it is very important to make sure you keep everything in perspective. Your willingness to seek the opinions of a friend can make all the difference. There are gains to be made by looking at things from another point of view.

8 MONDAY *Moon Age Day 14 Moon Sign Pisces*

Success today is about keeping your mind sharp, and this would be an ideal time for detailed work of any sort. Make the most of the opportunity to come to terms with issues that have confused you in the past. Social trends continue to look favourable, and some of the best possibilities are available as a result of a prospective journey.

9 TUESDAY *Moon Age Day 15 Moon Sign Pisces*

A phase of greater introspection and evaluation is now indicated, and there are good reasons to accept that you cannot always be active and outgoing. Once again, it pays to look at things closely, and to avoid pushing ahead with plans until you are certain in your own mind that they are going to work out well.

10 WEDNESDAY *Moon Age Day 16 Moon Sign Aries*

With the lunar low around today an element of disillusionment is possible, though if you realise what is going on in an astrological sense you should also be aware that this is a temporary matter. Why not stick to routines? These should suit you for the next couple of days, and help you to create a sense of security for yourself.

11 THURSDAY *Moon Age Day 17 Moon Sign Aries*

Be prepared to deal with any slight difficulties in relationships today. Even if you don't believe that the fault is yours, you need to appreciate that it takes two to tango. It's natural to jump to conclusions if you don't understand the behaviour of friends, but you need to bear in mind that you may not know all the circumstances.

12 FRIDAY *Moon Age Day 18 Moon Sign Aries*

Although the Moon is still in your opposite sign, this needn't prevent you from feeling positive about yourself and from making the best of impressions on the world at large. The focus is now on your willingness to enjoy yourself, and to put deep thinking to one side. The future is an unwritten book, and for the moment you should accept that it is so.

13 SATURDAY *Moon Age Day 19 Moon Sign Taurus*

You might be required to fall back on your own resources a little today. That's no bad thing, though it all depends on how you choose to deal with the situation. It can be difficult to listen to advice from people you haven't got on with in the past. Bear in mind that if what they say is valid, you should at least take note.

14 SUNDAY *Moon Age Day 20 Moon Sign Taurus*

You can now afford to view the fruits of recent efforts in a more positive light, though that won't necessarily prevent a few twists and turns in the way your mind is working. Make the most of opportunities to firm up material plans, but recognise that a certain amount of modification may be necessary if you really want to score successes socially.

15 MONDAY *Moon Age Day 21 Moon Sign Gemini*

Now is the time to get onside with people you know have some good ideas. Teamwork is especially well highlighted under present trends, and you shouldn't have to look far to find something extremely interesting to do. There is much to be said for seeking some fresh air around this time.

16 TUESDAY *Moon Age Day 22 Moon Sign Gemini*

There are good reasons to focus on making financial gains today, with some of these coming like a bolt from the blue. Jumping to conclusions in matters of love is all very well, but you run the risk of finding yourself in a slightly embarrassing position. Sometimes the things that are never said turn out to be the most significant.

17 WEDNESDAY *Moon Age Day 23 Moon Sign Cancer*

Such is your personal charm today that you can turn it on at just about any time. This might prove to be a distinct advantage in situations that demand more from you. When others find it difficult to come up with the goods, you can show that you are at your best. Libra can certainly afford to be firing on all cylinders at the moment.

18 THURSDAY *Moon Age Day 24 Moon Sign Cancer*

It is very important under present planetary trends to think before you act. Libra can be amongst the most impulsive of all the zodiac signs, and there's always a danger that you will leap into something you'll eventually regret. Seek opportunities to contact those you don't see too often but who are still very important to you.

19 FRIDAY *Moon Age Day 25 Moon Sign Cancer*

Whatever is holding you back at the moment deserves serious attention. In a couple of days the Sun moves into your solar first house, which encourages far more progressive tendencies and a desire to move forward. In some ways you are presently clearing the decks for action, even if this is subconscious.

20 SATURDAY *Moon Age Day 26 Moon Sign Leo*

What sets you apart at the moment is your tremendous creativity. You can extend this in a number of different directions, with particular emphasis being on the attention you pay to your appearance. This may be just the excuse you need for a shopping trip, and a complete change of style for Libra can't be ruled out.

21 SUNDAY *Moon Age Day 27 Moon Sign Leo*

It isn't what life shows on the surface that matters most today but rather the undertones. Bear in mind that what people say and what they mean could be very different things, and it's up to you to tell the difference. Turn up that famous intuition and do what you can to defuse any potential issues before they even appear.

22 MONDAY *Moon Age Day 28 Moon Sign Virgo*

It shouldn't take you long to bounce back from reversals, especially if you treat these as nothing more than phantoms. Your best approach is to greet today in a very cheerful frame of mind and to act with all the gusto that your zodiac sign possesses. Be prepared to give certain personal relationships more attention than usual.

23 TUESDAY *Moon Age Day 29 Moon Sign Virgo*

You have what it takes to remain generally happy and confident at the moment, even if the antics of a few people are trying your patience somewhat. What helps is your natural sense of humour, which although slightly 'off the wall' supports you through situations that would probably annoy others.

24 WEDNESDAY *Moon Age Day 0 Moon Sign Virgo*

There is more in the way of good luck available today, and you need to play this for all you are worth. Untypically, you can afford to pursue a gamble of some sort, though present trends discourage monetary risks. Speaking of finances, it's worth paying careful attention to documents during this week.

25 THURSDAY *Moon Age Day 1 Moon Sign Libra*

Today is favourable for all sorts of new plans and for consolidating past gains in original ways. The lunar high encourages a sociable approach, and assists you to show the flair you possess for organising almost anything. Your willingness to push forward on all fronts should prove that any negative traits of the last few days are nothing but a dull memory.

26 FRIDAY *Moon Age Day 2 Moon Sign Libra*

You now have scope to tap into a great deal of energy, and to turn this in whatever direction takes your fancy. Even if there isn't anything particularly important happening at present, you are in a favourable position to enjoy yourself, and also to bring a good deal of happiness into the lives of the people with whom you make contact.

27 SATURDAY *Moon Age Day 3 Moon Sign Scorpio*

Be aware of the strong personalities around you today, since you will have to be on form if you want to compete with them. Before you make life into any sort of competition, it might be sensible to ask yourself whether this is even necessary. Originality seems to be the best key to success both for today and for several more to come.

28 SUNDAY *Moon Age Day 4 Moon Sign Scorpio*

Current influences assist you to make plenty of progress, and in some cases much more than you expected. There are signs that the light of love is in your eyes, thanks to the present position of the planet Venus in your solar chart. Today is an ideal opportunity to heat up a particular relationship and to prove just how amorous you can be.

29 MONDAY *Moon Age Day 5 Moon Sign Sagittarius*

The start of a new working week can be a generally happy interlude, though your desire for fresh fields and pastures new is emphasised. It should now be possible for you to stretch credibility and to bring about the very alterations to your life that you seem to need the most. Your concern for the underdog is notable around now.

30 TUESDAY *Moon Age Day 6 Moon Sign Sagittarius*

You have everything you need to be right on the ball now when it comes to communicating, though of course there's nothing too strange about that as far as Libra is concerned. Keeping your interests topical counts for a great deal under present trends. Older Librans might even feel that they are coming back into fashion again – and without much effort!

October

2014

1 WEDNESDAY *Moon Age Day 7 Moon Sign Sagittarius*

There is now a major new focus on leisure and romantic matters. One benefit of getting things working well in general is that it enables you to appreciate the impression you are making on others. There are distinct gains to be made at this time from simply being what you naturally are. Personalities abound, both at work at socially.

2 THURSDAY *Moon Age Day 8 Moon Sign Capricorn*

Financial objectives can benefit from planetary assistance today, making this a favourable interlude to look at money and to work out how best to plan for the future. At the same time there is a strong social quality to the day, and you shouldn't have too much trouble in mixing business with pleasure.

3 FRIDAY *Moon Age Day 9 Moon Sign Capricorn*

Even if part of you wants to push forward progressively, there may be aspects of your mind that are restricted and far from forward-looking. Your willingness to take on board the needs of those close to you is a key ingredient in your efforts to enjoy a family day. Discussions can be useful, but avoid allowing them to lead to arguments.

4 SATURDAY *Moon Age Day 10 Moon Sign Aquarius*

The astrological trends around you favour progress on most fronts, assisting you to make any work in progress at the moment both rewarding and materially satisfying. It might sometimes be difficult to understand the motivations of those who are close to you, and a little probing could well be necessary in order to clarify things.

5 SUNDAY ☿ *Moon Age Day 11 Moon Sign Aquarius*

There ought to be plenty of ways you can feed your ego at the moment. After all, it isn't as large as is the case with some zodiac signs. It's natural to want to preen yourself now and again, and to appreciate how important you are to those around you. Fishing for compliments might allow you to land you a bigger than expected catch today!

6 MONDAY ☿ *Moon Age Day 12 Moon Sign Pisces*

This would be an auspicious time to push ahead with any sort of fresh start you have been contemplating, or any improvements and changes you want to make at home. Enlisting the support of family members in the planning stage would be no bad thing, but at the end of the day it's really a case of taking the bull by the horns.

7 TUESDAY ☿ *Moon Age Day 13 Moon Sign Pisces*

Even if this part of the working week is fast and furious, you need to be prepared to slow things down considerably tomorrow. This will be the legacy of the lunar low, and if you realise that fact now, you have a chance to put a few matters on hold in advance of the quieter interlude.

8 WEDNESDAY ☿ *Moon Age Day 14 Moon Sign Aries*

This would not be the best time in which to make any major decisions. On the contrary, the lunar low encourages you to hold yourself back somewhat, and you may decide that the best option is to spend at least a few hours on your own. None of this has any bearing on your creativity, which shows itself strongly at the moment.

9 THURSDAY ☿ *Moon Age Day 15 Moon Sign Aries*

Libra can afford to be a little self-indulgent and even quite inward-looking today. Your idea of being selfish is simply spending a little time on your own and there is nothing wrong with that. In any case, it provides an opportunity to come up with some new ideas, which you can act upon under the more progressive trends tomorrow.

10 FRIDAY ☿ *Moon Age Day 16 Moon Sign Taurus*

Social encounters offer plenty of potential rewards today, and will probably be more interesting than concentrating on the strictly practical aspects of life, some of which may be downright boring! Confidence remains essentially high, and if anyone tries to deflate you, you need to ask yourself whether this is down to jealousy.

11 SATURDAY ☿ *Moon Age Day 17 Moon Sign Taurus*

New opportunities for growth and expansion are within your reach at the present time. Trends indicate that you have the Midas touch at the moment, but that still doesn't mean you should be taking too many financial risks. As the day wears on a slightly quieter, more contemplative approach is indicated for Libra.

12 SUNDAY ☿ *Moon Age Day 18 Moon Sign Gemini*

It's time to put the more competitive side of your nature firmly on display and push forward on all fronts. This might not be especially easy, and you will need to use that extra bit of effort that is necessary to get ahead of any small difficulties you encounter. Acting on impulse comes as second nature under current planetary influences.

13 MONDAY ☿ *Moon Age Day 19 Moon Sign Gemini*

Success today is about your willingness to work hard and to do whatever it takes to get to your chosen destination. Rather than getting bogged down with details today, your best approach is to stick to the main themes of life because it's the big picture that counts. By the evening you have scope to find happiness and in the bosom of your family.

14 TUESDAY ☿ *Moon Age Day 20 Moon Sign Cancer*

Capitalise on the boost to your ego that is on offer now, perhaps as a result of the compliments that you are able to attract at the moment. The more you mix with the world at large, the greater are the potential rewards you can obtain. Even if your attention is somewhat divided at the moment, that needn't prevent you from concentrating.

15 WEDNESDAY ☿ *Moon Age Day 21 Moon Sign Cancer*

Monetary stability is well marked now, assisting you to look at things with a greater degree of certainty. There is real scope available for building on the successes of the past, and you can persuade other people to put their shoulders to the wheel on your behalf. Confidence gradually grows across today and tomorrow.

16 THURSDAY ☿ *Moon Age Day 22 Moon Sign Cancer*

Be prepared to cut your losses regarding a current project in order to make the very best of what lies in store for later. Arrangements for the weekend can be made today, especially if you are looking towards an important social gathering of some sort. It's important to take into account the feelings of those who are close to you today.

17 FRIDAY ☿ *Moon Age Day 23 Moon Sign Leo*

An ideal day for in-depth discussions, though how much they are worth remains to be seen. In the main there are good reasons to spend at least short periods of time on your own, or in the company of those you love and trust. By tomorrow any slight negative trends will be out of the way, so it pays to remain patient.

18 SATURDAY ☿ *Moon Age Day 24 Moon Sign Leo*

Your personality now seems stronger, giving you everything you need to take the weekend by storm if you choose. There are possible high spots on offer in terms of gatherings, particularly if you are able to mix with the sort of people you find both interesting and inspirational. Even previously awkward types might seem entertaining.

19 SUNDAY ☿ *Moon Age Day 25 Moon Sign Virgo*

Ridding yourself of any situation that seems to be holding you back would be a positive step now. You would be wise to sit and think about such matters before you take action, because present astrological trends encourage a slightly impulsive tendency. Nevertheless, once you have made up your mind, go for it!

20 MONDAY ☿ *Moon Age Day 26 Moon Sign Virgo*

Professional communications with colleagues or superiors are emphasised at present, and you make best use of this period by laying down plans for what might turn out to be a major professional coup. Meanwhile, romance is also well accented, with some Librans definitely spoiled for choice at the moment.

21 TUESDAY ☿ *Moon Age Day 27 Moon Sign Virgo*

A slightly quieter day suits the present interlude, but things will soon change and this evening you can start tapping into a greater sense of urgency and energy. In the meantime, it pays to clear the decks for action and to set things up both at work and socially. Don't be surprised if you find certain individuals difficult to read now.

22 WEDNESDAY ☿ *Moon Age Day 28 Moon Sign Libra*

Positive thinking really does pay off well today. The fact is that with the lunar high assisting you to bring so much light and energy into your life, virtually nothing is beyond your capabilities. Now would be a favourable time to address anything that has been at the back of your mind and which has been troubling you of late.

23 THURSDAY ☿ *Moon Age Day 0 Moon Sign Libra*

The positive trends continue, giving you every encouragement to stretch your mind in all sorts of new directions at the moment. It appears that your capacity for hard work is noteworthy, but you might not even notice the effort. Social trends also benefit, and time spent out and about with friends could prove exciting.

24 FRIDAY ☿ *Moon Age Day 1 Moon Sign Scorpio*

Trends are around that assist you to use your powers of attraction, and this indicates a time during which you should be ready to act on significant information. You may well already have a part of your mind set on matters for even later in the year, and might even be thinking about a change of scenery around Christmas.

25 SATURDAY ☿ *Moon Age Day 2 Moon Sign Scorpio*

Communication has a great deal to offer, so this is not a good time for keeping quiet. All the same, your interests are best served by taking a listening approach rather than always pushing your own point of view. This is not simply a matter of being diplomatic, as it offers you scope to collect ideas that you may want to adopt as your own.

26 SUNDAY *Moon Age Day 3 Moon Sign Scorpio*

Love and romance look particularly hopeful for Libra now. Personal attachments can help you to put a smile on your face and you know how to get the best out of any sort of relationship. It's time to use a combination of your natural charm, together with your ability to make anyone feel as if they are very important.

27 MONDAY *Moon Age Day 4 Moon Sign Sagittarius*

Today marks a period during which communicating well with colleagues can really pay dividends. Co-operative matters are especially well starred and this is definitely not a go-it-alone sort of period. Even if you find routines quite tedious, you can find ways to make them go with a swing and to get the most out of them.

28 TUESDAY *Moon Age Day 5 Moon Sign Sagittarius*

For much of the month you have had room to make reasonable progress in material matters, and now comes a time when it's worth consolidating all your efforts up to now. Some ingenuity may be required, and you also need to be fairly definite in your actions. That might not seem like much, but it's very important to Libra.

29 WEDNESDAY *Moon Age Day 6 Moon Sign Capricorn*

Material duties may limit your possibilities today, and if this is the case you probably won't feel yourself to have the freedom you would wish. It may be difficult to make this the most startling day of the month generally, but there are gains if you look for them. Your best approach is to stick to things you already know you are good at.

30 THURSDAY *Moon Age Day 7 Moon Sign Capricorn*

Emotional issues you haven't been able to remedy could be the source of your discontent today. If you can stay away from these, generally speaking the world should be your oyster. You have what it takes to come out of the fog that has surrounded your decision-making for a few days, and to create a clear picture of the future.

31 FRIDAY *Moon Age Day 8 Moon Sign Aquarius*

Getting well on top of most practical issues today enables you to focus more on enjoyment. If you haven't exactly been painting the town red of late, now is the time to put that right. Make the most of any opportunities to discover the true feelings of someone who's been very special to you for a long time.

November 2014

1 SATURDAY *Moon Age Day 9 Moon Sign Aquarius*

Where practical interests are concerned, there's an indication that you may be rather short-sighted at present, which is why it would be sensible to seek the opinions of more experienced individuals. You can't be an expert at everything, and if you have done favours for others in the past, you shouldn't be afraid to call one or two of them in now.

2 SUNDAY *Moon Age Day 10 Moon Sign Pisces*

At this time there is potential for great harmony in and around your home, so this might seem to be the best place to be. Although you are probably right, you shouldn't ignore any issues in the outside world that still demand your attention. Under these circumstances, getting any real peace and quiet may not be at all easy. Take matters in your stride.

3 MONDAY *Moon Age Day 11 Moon Sign Pisces*

The focus today is on your ability to fulfil demands of various kinds. You can't expect everything to be quite as secure as you wish, though if life keeps you guessing that can add exactly the sort of spice you like. There are no easy ways to success right now, but having to surmount obstacles enables you to enjoy the results all the more.

4 TUESDAY *Moon Age Day 12 Moon Sign Aries*

With the lunar low now in evidence, it's important to avoid reacting in a negative way to situations that are clearly temporary. By all means give yourself fully to the task at hand, but don't expect to push down every barrier around now. Social trends are well accented, especially in terms of mixing with people you already know and like.

5 WEDNESDAY *Moon Age Day 13 Moon Sign Aries*

If your capacity for getting ahead is still less than you would wish, a certain amount of frustration could be the result. Patience is called for, at a time when you don't seem to have much. Creative powers remain undiminished, however, making this an ideal time to embark on practical projects that require a steady approach.

6 THURSDAY *Moon Age Day 14 Moon Sign Taurus*

There are favourable trends available for financial dealings of any sort at the moment, though you would be wise to keep your eyes open for people and situations that are not quite what they seem. It's important to read the small print carefully before entering into any sort of binding commitment. A day to be on your guard generally.

7 FRIDAY *Moon Age Day 15 Moon Sign Taurus*

A great sense of both fulfilment and security is on offer for Libra at the moment, encouraging you to stay close to home and family when you can. If the attitudes of some of your colleagues are making work a less than wonderful experience, your best approach is simply to focus as best you can on whatever else is going on in your life.

8 SATURDAY *Moon Age Day 16 Moon Sign Taurus*

Be prepared to make full use of a continuing trend that has a strong bearing on money matters. Part of your success during the current interlude is your willingness to accept help and support from other people, whether or not you have asked for it. You need to be sure of yourself before taking any sort of risk.

9 SUNDAY *Moon Age Day 17 Moon Sign Gemini*

You can now afford to branch out on your own, and have what it takes to make significant headway in directions that you didn't expect. There is much about today that seems distinctly original, and it's up to you to respond positively to new offers that are available. There's little point in getting involved in discussions that lead nowhere.

10 MONDAY *Moon Age Day 18 Moon Sign Gemini*

The focus is on your determination to make outright progress, especially at work. If you are between jobs at the moment, this ought to be a good time to keep your eyes and ears open. It's flattering if people want to do you favours, though that doesn't necessarily mean that all of their offers of help will be particularly welcome.

11 TUESDAY *Moon Age Day 19 Moon Sign Cancer*

Current trends suggest that you may need to streamline your life in some way at the moment. Beware of spending more money than is necessary, especially on things that you don't really want or need at all. A settled and happy time is available in the company of family members, though the influence of strangers may not be quite as positive just now.

12 WEDNESDAY *Moon Age Day 20 Moon Sign Cancer*

It's time to put your mind to work and take care of any details that need to be sorted. The more you get done early in the day, the better is the prospect for social happiness later on. This would not be a good time to argue for your limitations, especially at work. There's nothing wrong with believing that you can do almost anything!

13 THURSDAY *Moon Age Day 21 Moon Sign Leo*

Communications are now in your best interest and there is very little point in sitting in a corner and waiting for life to come to you. Once again the focus is on family matters. Be prepared to offer congratulations where these are due, and make the most of the chance to make a special fuss of relatives who have done well of late.

14 FRIDAY *Moon Age Day 22 Moon Sign Leo*

Your personality sparkles around now, assisting you to discover lots of possibilities waiting in the wings. In some ways this is the most fortunate time of the month because of your levels of energy and your desire to please others. You can't expect this to work in every single case. After all, you are not a miracle-worker.

15 SATURDAY *Moon Age Day 23 Moon Sign Leo*

Wanting to have the last word in discussions is all very well, though it could prove to be something of an irritant to others. Bear in mind that Christmas is just around the corner and be ready to undertake some forward planning. There are worse medium-term objectives that that of gathering your family around you.

16 SUNDAY *Moon Age Day 24 Moon Sign Virgo*

You can now take positive action to expand your financial horizons, and could make gains as a result of the actions of others. Even if you are looking closely at money, this doesn't necessarily have to be the entire motivation of your life at the moment. Close, personal ties are also on the agenda, and you should be doing what you can to strengthen them.

17 MONDAY *Moon Age Day 25 Moon Sign Virgo*

Financial and business trends could well be a slightly mixed bag. The spotlight is on a distinctly unsettled element at the moment, and it may be difficult for you to feel totally comfortable in any specific way. Confidence should grow as the day progresses, but trying to move any mountains is unlikely to be on your agenda right now.

18 TUESDAY *Moon Age Day 26 Moon Sign Libra*

The lunar high offers you plenty of opportunity to redress the balance and fits you for great things today. At this stage of the week you should be keen to get on, and should be pushing the bounds of the possible whenever you can. You can't expect to get everyone on your side, so it's worth concentrating on the people who really matter.

19 WEDNESDAY *Moon Age Day 27 Moon Sign Libra*

This would be an excellent period for telling others how things really are. Even if you have been slightly shy of facing up to a specific individual, you're encouraged to overcome that today. Stand up for what you believe to be true and you may be surprised at just how willingly others defer to your opinion.

20 THURSDAY *Moon Age Day 28 Moon Sign Libra*

Be ready to make the most of potentially pleasurable social events around now, even if you are also quite busy at work. There are gains to be made from simply watching and waiting, whilst at other times it is actions that count. Knowing the difference is really down to your very strong intuition, which is heightened under present influences.

21 FRIDAY *Moon Age Day 29 Moon Sign Scorpio*

It's sensible to leave room for new plans and schemes because you have plenty of scope to make things happen at the moment, and need to be on the ball if you want to make the most of this interlude. If you need to do something you hate, your best approach is to get it out of the way as early in the day as possible.

22 SATURDAY *Moon Age Day 0 Moon Sign Scorpio*

This is not the best day of month to be gambling, but if you really must take a chance it is important that your risks are very calculated. Some limitations are placed upon you by life itself and you have to realise that it isn't always possible to get exactly what you want. Your ability to stay cool in tight situations really counts now.

23 SUNDAY *Moon Age Day 1 Moon Sign Sagittarius*

There may be little double that you are mentally alert and anxious to do whatever it takes to prove yourself, though the best trends today are definitely personal ones. Attitude is very important when it comes to getting the best from romance, and there's nothing wrong with overblown gestures such as chocolates, flowers – or a ticket to the next match!

24 MONDAY *Moon Age Day 2 Moon Sign Sagittarius*

A good lift is now available to you where one-to-one relationships are concerned, and it's worth concentrating plenty of your effort on securing and maintaining positive relationships. You could do worse than to heap attention on your partner or the person you care for the most. This evening could prove particularly opportune for love.

25 TUESDAY *Moon Age Day 3 Moon Sign Capricorn*

Make arrangements now, because there are signs that your organisational skills are about as good as they have been at any time during November. Even if it is hard to bring others round to your way of thinking, make the most of the fact that you are very much under the influence of some positive planetary associations.

26 WEDNESDAY *Moon Age Day 4 Moon Sign Capricorn*

Inspiration is there for the taking right now, and it's time to put the unconventional side of your nature clearly on display. Your best option is to try for a very different sort of day and to take other people on the ride with you. This is not an ideal interlude for sticking around at home wearing your slippers.

27 THURSDAY *Moon Age Day 5 Moon Sign Aquarius*

This is not a good day to be making comparisons. It's important to realise that you are what you are, and as such have your own individual characteristics. It doesn't matter how much you admire a particular person, you can't change your nature to be exactly the same as they are. Show that you are proud to be yourself.

28 FRIDAY *Moon Age Day 6 Moon Sign Aquarius*

The forthright and challenging side of the Libra nature is emphasised, encouraging you not to take anything for granted, but rather to turn over every stone in life to see what lies beneath it. This is admirable in one way, but you need to bear in mind how others will view it. Being considered interfering may not be helpful in the longer term.

29 SATURDAY *Moon Age Day 7 Moon Sign Pisces*

You can't expect everyone to respond in the way you wish, and you need to be as flexible as possible if you want to make the most of what is available right now. Romance is the key to the greatest sense of happiness that surrounds you today. For some Libran people that might involve responding to overtures from surprising directions.

30 SUNDAY *Moon Age Day 8 Moon Sign Pisces*

This is a Sunday on which talking to family members could prove very useful, especially anyone who seems to have been out of sorts recently. If congratulations are in the offing somewhere in your social circle, there are good reasons to make sure you are the first at the front of the queue to offer them.

December

2014

1 MONDAY *Moon Age Day 9 Moon Sign Pisces*

If you are involved in important meetings of any sort today, it would be sensible to rehearse what you are going to say instead of shooting from the hip. Libra is rarely impetuous, but an element of this trait is indicated under present astrological trends. Personalities could well predominate as far as your social life is concerned.

2 TUESDAY *Moon Age Day 10 Moon Sign Aries*

Whether you like it or not the Moon has moved into your opposite zodiac sign, suggesting that a couple of quieter days would be no bad thing. This isn't easy because other planetary positions and aspects are pushing you forward. Being caught between the devil and the deep blue sea is something you have to cope with.

3 WEDNESDAY *Moon Age Day 11 Moon Sign Aries*

Keeping a fairly low profile is the name of the game today. This doesn't mean you have to put a damper on things for others, though your own progress may be a little below par. Routines have a great deal to offer now, and there is happiness to be found in your home environment. By the evening you might be feeling on better form.

4 THURSDAY *Moon Age Day 12 Moon Sign Taurus*

The emphasis at the moment is on a broad-minded outlook, which is not so unusual for your zodiac sign. Once again, routines can be very useful, but at the same time you should now look well ahead and notice the stimulating potential of what lies before you in more than one area of life.

5 FRIDAY *Moon Age Day 13 Moon Sign Taurus*

Work issues are particularly well accented at the moment, despite the possibility that your level of efficiency in a general sense is not quite as high as would usually be the case. Realising that Christmas is now so close might not help, particularly if there is still a great deal to get done, in amongst a busy schedule.

6 SATURDAY *Moon Age Day 14 Moon Sign Gemini*

There are many priorities to be dealt with just now, and once again you could discover that time is of the essence. Why not pass some of these tasks to other people? You have what it takes to persuade friends in particular to lend a hand and to do whatever they can to lessen your burden in life.

7 SUNDAY *Moon Age Day 15 Moon Sign Gemini*

Financially speaking you can now capitalise on more positive trends. Of course you can't guarantee that any minor gains made at the moment will continue for too long, because the approach of Christmas is often a time for some extra spending. Take every opportunity to wallow in life's little luxuries now if you can.

8 MONDAY *Moon Age Day 16 Moon Sign Cancer*

Versatility seems to be the chief key to success around now, and it is what will enable you to keep up with the general flow of life. Be ready to respond to any small stumbling blocks you encounter at work, though in the main you have the ability to make more than steady progress, and to tap into positive social trends.

9 TUESDAY *Moon Age Day 17 Moon Sign Cancer*

Even if you feel you are pretty much on target with regard to your broad aims in life, the quieter side of your nature could now be the source of a few minor setbacks. Maybe you don't have quite the level of confidence to get things running your way, whether practically or financially. The answer is easy – enlist some support!

10 WEDNESDAY *Moon Age Day 18 Moon Sign Cancer*

Today is about your ability to deal with the pressures coming in from the outside world and your willingness commit yourself fully to what lies ahead in terms of the celebrations. Librans generally love the run-up to Christmas, even if a few of you try to pretend that this is not the case. You can afford to socialise whenever possible.

11 THURSDAY *Moon Age Day 19 Moon Sign Leo*

There is much to be said for spending time thinking about and planning for your social life at the moment. Although there are small gains to be made in the more practical aspects of your life, you should also be looking for opportunities to allow your mind to focus on less concrete issues.

12 FRIDAY *Moon Age Day 20 Moon Sign Leo*

If you are prepared to take on board all the interesting things that are available at present, there probably won't be enough time to take it all in! In terms of communication, you are in a very mercurial state of mind, and this assists you to mix freely with all sorts of people. You can't expect all your acquaintances to approve of one another.

13 SATURDAY *Moon Age Day 21 Moon Sign Virgo*

It's time to put your best qualities on display and ensure that today proves to be both rewarding and interesting. Risk-taking is on the agenda, even if these are fairly calculated gambles. Keeping one eye on the Christmas period is a good idea, and in many respects this is the time when you can really begin to get yourself into a festive mood.

14 SUNDAY *Moon Age Day 22 Moon Sign Virgo*

You may not feel like taking on the whole world at the moment, even if your levels of energy are actually fairly high. The Moon is in your solar twelfth house, enhancing the very contemplative aspect of your nature. Thinking carefully before you embark on anything major is certainly not a waste of time.

15 MONDAY *Moon Age Day 23 Moon Sign Virgo*

Once again, a slower approach is now the order of the day, and that should leave you some time to stand and think about life. This is a positive exercise for you now and again, and it can lead to some startling realisations. Most of the time you are too busy living your life to actually work out whether your direction is the right one.

16 TUESDAY *Moon Age Day 24 Moon Sign Libra*

The lunar high assists you to maintain a very happy frame of mind and to have a go at anything – even things you have turned your nose up at in the past. Who knows, you might enjoy yourself much more than you expected. Even if you don't, there's a certain satisfaction in having got involved, and in bringing joy to other people.

17 WEDNESDAY *Moon Age Day 25 Moon Sign Libra*

You can successfully broaden the number of social contacts who are important to your life now and who could play an even bigger part later. Doing half a dozen different things at the same time should come as second nature to you, and you need to look out for the chance to make some financial gains that are basically down to luck.

18 THURSDAY *Moon Age Day 26 Moon Sign Scorpio*

Practical matters should be running smoothly enough, and you have a chance to contribute a very joyful attitude to whatever is going on around you at this time. Today would be favourable for organising and for getting an overview of where you are at the moment. There ought to be time for extreme activity – and for relaxation too!

19 FRIDAY *Moon Age Day 27 Moon Sign Scorpio*

The question now is whether you can find the right kind of opportunities necessary to get ahead. Even little chances should be seized upon, giving you the impetus you need to make progress in the professional stakes and enjoy better luck generally. Although you might be in the mood to take a gamble, a little care would still be advisable.

20 SATURDAY *Moon Age Day 28 Moon Sign Sagittarius*

Everyday matters have the potential to keep you busy this weekend, but that needn't stop you from finding time to get together with friends, especially if there are occasions that could provide plenty of entertainment. The weekend ought to offer you the chance to stop and take stock, but that doesn't rule out having a good time as well.

21 SUNDAY *Moon Age Day 29 Moon Sign Sagittarius*

Ask yourself whether social groups with which you haven't been associated before could now prove important in your life now, and be prepared to widen your horizons whenever possible. There mightn't be very much time for rest, and even if this doesn't bother you too much personally, it's worth giving some thought to your partner and family members.

22 MONDAY *Moon Age Day 0 Moon Sign Sagittarius*

The planetary emphasis today is mainly on domestic matters, and for this reason you may decide to put practical and professional matters on the back burner for a little while. The social maelstrom that is Christmas is already beginning, but there's nothing wrong with taking a rain check regarding at least some of the festivities, especially today and tomorrow.

23 TUESDAY *Moon Age Day 1 Moon Sign Capricorn*

Ask yourself whether any difficulties between yourself and your partner have more to do with pressures from the outside world than with personal disagreements. It would be good to look at things from a distance and not to allow the world at large to impinge on your deepest attachments. Your willingness to seek relaxation can make all the difference today.

24 WEDNESDAY *Moon Age Day 2 Moon Sign Capricorn*

Social relationships start to offer bigger and better times, and it's time for you to show that you can turn heads. Whatever the beliefs of others, you have what it takes to succeed in matters that haven't been your forte before, and your consistent commitment should be there for all to see. This should be an excellent Christmas Eve.

25 THURSDAY *Moon Age Day 3 Moon Sign Aquarius*

Today has much to offer you, particularly if you are determined to remain happy and confident as you embark on the Christmas festivities. Being naturally caring and giving, you can get a great deal of your own joy from helping others to have a good time. Be prepared to share yourself between your partner, family and friends.

26 FRIDAY *Moon Age Day 4 Moon Sign Aquarius*

If you feel it is necessary to make some slight changes to an aspect of your personal life, you needn't be short of advice on this score. Find friends who are willing to share their wisdom with you, even if you are unsure how much they actually know. In the end it comes down to whether or not you would prefer to suit yourself.

27 SATURDAY *Moon Age Day 5 Moon Sign Pisces*

Mental stimulation is the key for this weekend. If you allow yourself to get so bogged down with boring routines that you have no time to think, this is unlikely to produce good results. Libra is very ingenious at the best of times, but that ingenuity could be going off the scale today. It's time to show others your most charismatic and attractive side.

28 SUNDAY *Moon Age Day 6 Moon Sign Pisces*

A slightly more independent approach is now the name of the game, though this could be somewhat stifled if you feel you can't get on with things. That's the nature of the Christmas holidays, because even if you are in the mood to keep moving, you can't guarantee that others share your enthusiasm. Keep a sense of proportion where money is concerned.

29 MONDAY *Moon Age Day 7 Moon Sign Aries*

Your interests are best served by getting rid of situations that are not doing you any good at all, and the lunar low offers you an opportunity to do this. This is certainly a favourable time for clearing the decks for action that you are planning for later, and may well be the last chance you have to do so before the New Year arrives.

30 TUESDAY *Moon Age Day 8 Moon Sign Aries*

Practical matters could be a little fraught under current influences, particularly if you insist on trying to do too many things at the same time. There are possible gains in a romantic sense, though even here you might find it slightly tricky to understand the behaviour and attitude of your partner or sweetheart. Be willing to stop and think carefully today.

31 WEDNESDAY *Moon Age Day 9 Moon Sign Taurus*

Domestic issues continue to offer you scope for fulfilment, and new social influences may help you to lighten the load if you feel that certain jobs are getting you down a little. With the New Year celebrations in view, there's even a suggestion that you may be tiring of having a good time. An organised approach is the key to success at the moment.

RISING SIGNS FOR LIBRA

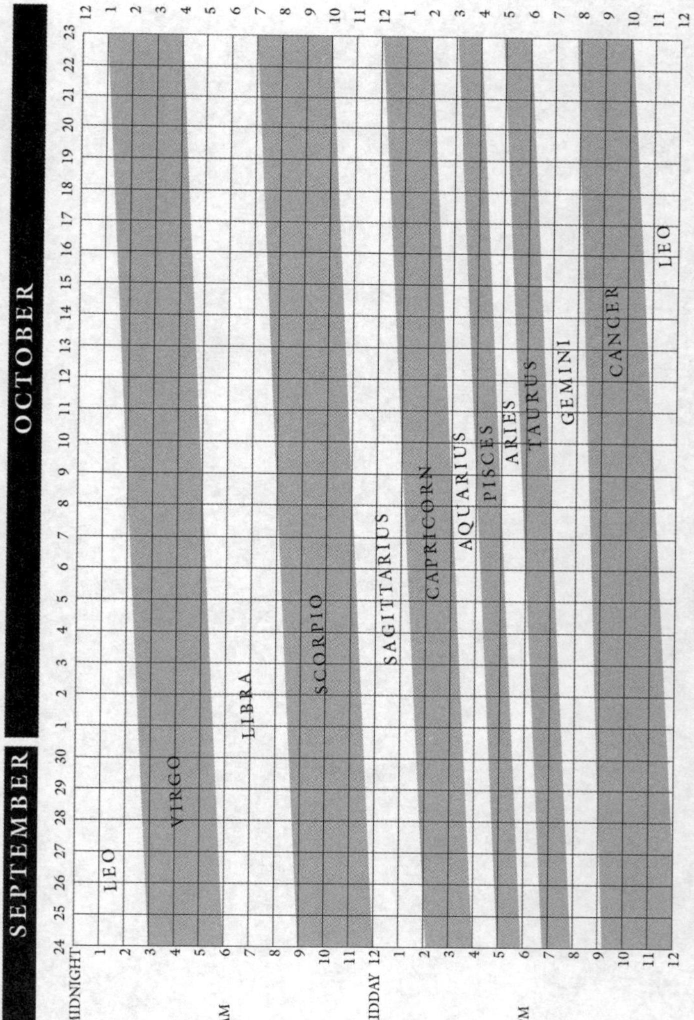

THE ZODIAC, PLANETS AND CORRESPONDENCES

The Earth revolves around the Sun once every calendar year, so when viewed from Earth the Sun appears in a different part of the sky as the year progresses. In astrology, these parts of the sky are divided into the signs of the zodiac and this means that the signs are organised in a circle. The circle begins with Aries and ends with Pisces.

Taking the zodiac sign as a starting point, astrologers then work with all the positions of planets, stars and many other factors to calculate horoscopes and birth charts and tell us what the stars have in store for us.

The table below shows the planets and Elements for each of the signs of the zodiac. Each sign belongs to one of the four Elements: Fire, Air, Earth or Water. Fire signs are creative and enthusiastic; Air signs are mentally active and thoughtful; Earth signs are constructive and practical; Water signs are emotional and have strong feelings.

It also shows the metals and gemstones associated with, or corresponding with, each sign. The correspondence is made when a metal or stone possesses properties that are held in common with a particular sign of the zodiac.

Finally, the table shows the opposite of each star sign – this is the opposite sign in the astrological circle.

Placed	Sign	Symbol	Element	Planet	Metal	Stone	Opposite
1	Aries	Ram	Fire	Mars	Iron	Bloodstone	Libra
2	Taurus	Bull	Earth	Venus	Copper	Sapphire	Scorpio
3	Gemini	Twins	Air	Mercury	Mercury	Tiger's Eye	Sagittarius
4	Cancer	Crab	Water	Moon	Silver	Pearl	Capricorn
5	Leo	Lion	Fire	Sun	Gold	Ruby	Aquarius
6	Virgo	Maiden	Earth	Mercury	Mercury	Sardonyx	Pisces
7	Libra	Scales	Air	Venus	Copper	Sapphire	Aries
8	Scorpio	Scorpion	Water	Pluto	Plutonium	Jasper	Taurus
9	Sagittarius	Archer	Fire	Jupiter	Tin	Topaz	Gemini
10	Capricorn	Goat	Earth	Saturn	Lead	Black Onyx	Cancer
11	Aquarius	Waterbearer	Air	Uranus	Uranium	Amethyst	Leo
12	Pisces	Fishes	Water	Neptune	Tin	Moonstone	Virgo